Doughn
for
Urban
Development

A Manual

Published in 2023 by The Danish Architectural Press with support from Realdania

Foreword

Hello reader
The aim of this book is to provide developers and other building industry actors with a manual that supports the application and practice of Doughnut principles in urban development. Within, is the outcome of two years of collaborative work.

To solve the climate crisis, we need to systematically change the way we live, design, and regenerate our systems and thereby society. To enable this change we must work together in new ways, which is why we brought together a dream team with diverse, sometimes even opposing points of view, to present a holistic approach to urban development. The co-creating team behind the Doughnut for Urban Development accounts for more than twenty content authors and an additional twenty contributing experts who have invested in this project because we share a common goal and hope for the future.

We share a sense of urgency for climate action and believe in creating a new socio-economic and planetary paradigm. In this book we create a sector focused blueprint for how to apply Doughnut Economics in practice. With that, it is important to underline that this is not a certification scheme or an extensive to-do list for companies to operate a "doughnut company" but rather a manual and framework for steering the building industry towards a safe and just space for humanity to thrive, within the means of the planet's limited natural resources.

What's new
This book is an extension of the Doughnut as we know it and the findings throughout can be considered as incremental additions by applying the Doughnut in sectoral practice. To make new contributions we've brought together the fields of climate science, impact assessment, ecology and building design to create new understandings. In our multidisciplinary and multinational team, we participated in three key workshops that shaped the content. We started in Copenhagen with a 'Doughnut Unrolled' workshop to understand the Doughnut's four lenses which helped shape the scope of the project. We then met in London where we unrolled the social foundation and took a deep dive into the world of social impact assessment. Finally, we met in Stockholm to unroll the ecological foundation and glean the latest scientific insights from the Planetary Boundaries framework. Through these workshops, steering committee meetings and content focused subgroups we came to some novel insights.

Measuring social impact
We started with a mission to quantify and assign absolute measures to the social foundation. We quickly found out that doing so was not possible, not least, desirable. Rather, we focused our attention on defining social impact areas by local and global dimensions recognising the context sensitivity of such social dimensions.

Allocation for buildings
The planetary boundary for climate change is well defined and thus relatively easy to measure. Scaling down that boundary to the urban development level is less straightforward. Allocation is not just a mathematical science but rather a subjective and inherently political pursuit. Many of the known allocation principles such as equal per capita, historical responsibility and grandfathering, perpetuate business-as-usual and the growth dependent economic paradigm of today.

In pursuit of defining an allocation principle more aligned with Doughnut's distributive principle we present in this book an emerging sharing principle of sufficiency, which is based on the fulfilment of human needs. The result of this exploration is an informed discourse about how we might scale building industry operations within planetary limits and the indisputable fact that we must urgently reduce climate impact.

Two planetary systems

In our work with the Stockholm Resilience Centre, we discovered that there are two core Earth systems to which all planetary boundaries relate - climate stability and healthy ecosystems - both measurable and specific through Earth science. With this knowledge, we can now focus our innovation pursuits with two key objectives: We need to set and comply with carbon budgets in our building projects to scale impact within planetary limits, while at the same time we need to protect, support and regenerate nature and biodiversity.

Measuring biodiversity

We have learned about how to use the biodiversity net gain framework to mitigate the impact of urban development on site, through regenerative measures to create more diverse and thriving biotopes. We worked to expand the scope of biodiversity loss across the global supply chain and have created a 'Off-site Biodiversity Tool' for measuring indirect impacts of urban development on ecosystem health.

Deep business design

In our work with Doughnut Economics Action Lab, it became clear that Doughnut Economics in practice needs to be supported with more than goals and targets. It depends deeply on the nature of business structure. As such, current businesses designed for the pursuit of economic growth need to be redesigned to unlock transformative actions in their purpose, through networks, financial parameters, ownership and governance structures.

These findings are unfolded in the five chapters of this book and presented here as key learnings you can use in urban development work.

Doughnut Economics: a compass to guide urban development

In this chapter, we set the scene. The Doughnut aims to steer civilisation towards the Doughnut of social and planetary boundaries. The inner ring, the social foundation represents the minimum social standards required for human well-being, while the outer ring, the ecological ceiling represents the ecological limits of the planet. The 'Doughnut principles of practice' and the 'Unrolling methodology' are presented as useful frameworks that can be applied to steer urban development towards the space between the social foundation and ecological ceiling - a doughnut-shaped safe and just space for humanity in a global context. Finally, we present the Doughnut for Urban Development.

The Social Foundation for Urban Development

In the second chapter we introduce the inner ring, the social foundation of the Doughnut for Urban Development. This chapter can be used to better understand how frameworks such as the UN 17 Sustainable Development Goals and EU Taxonomy, can be applied to scale global ambitions and apply them directly to urban development. It focuses on four essential categories: connectedness, inclusivity, equity, and responsibility, highlighting their relevance and impact on urban development. We present the background and methodology behind defining the social foundation, which concludes in presenting 24 local and 24 global social impact areas.

The Ecological Ceiling for Urban Development

In the third chapter we introduce the outer ring, the ecological ceiling of the Doughnut for Urban Development. This chapter can be used to better understand how the Planetary Boundaries framework can be used to scale planetary limits down to impact areas relevant for urban development within two categories: climate stability and healthy ecosystem. We present the background and methodology behind defining the ecological ceiling, which concludes in presenting 24 local and 24 global ecological impact areas.

Urban Development within Planetary Boundaries

In this chapter, we focus on methods for urban developments to set planetary targets that respect climate stability and healthy ecosystems, and to measure ecological performance – on-site and off-site – using approaches such as life cycle assessment (LCA) and 'Biodiversity Net Gain.' This chapter can be used as a tool to learn about setting measurable, evidence-based targets to scale urban development within planetary boundaries with the goal of creating regenerative outcomes.

Doughnut Design for Business

In this chapter, we introduce the idea that for a business to pursue regenerative outcomes it should also look inward at its business design. We present the 'Doughnut Design for Business' tool which emphasizes five key deep design features: Purpose, Networks, Governance, Ownership, and Finance. Finally, we include a case study on Home.Earth and the business design features embraced in pursuit of regenerative outcomes. This chapter can be used to transform your organization on its journey to pursue social and planetary well-being.

There's more

We don't believe in copy rights, but in the right to copy. We truly hope this publication will serve as inspiration for the decision makers and the practitioners of urban development. In addition to this manual, we have created resources which are open-sourced and available for free to support you on your journey towards applying Doughnut principles in urban development, which can be found at the end of this book. The additional resources include a digital download of this manual, an Appendix which supports the science presented in this manual, a Database which details the 48 social and 48 ecological impact areas defined in this manual, and a Toolkit to facilitate the adaptation and application of the Doughnut for Urban Development in your next urban development project.

Finally...

We know this manual is neither perfect nor exhaustive. Most likely, some of the content will already be outdated by the time you read this passage. However, we know that when applied the principles presented in this book can lead to regenerative urban development. We know that change is about progress, not perfection. It's about inspiration, transparency, and action. Building on Doughnut Economics and the Planetary Boundaries framework is an honour. Translating these well-known and revered works into the urban development context has been complex and exciting. We believe in the Doughnut vision for the future and have done our best to bring that to life. Generous, regenerative, distributive, and irresistible.

Let's get to work!

Dani Hill-Hansen and Kasper Guldager Jensen
Copenhagen, June 2023

Kate Raworth,
Co-founder and Conceptual Lead, DEAL

Kate provides conceptual leadership on Doughnut Economics, within the team and in the emerging community of practitioners and presents DEAL's ideas and work internationally. She is an economist and the author of the international best-seller Doughnut Economics: seven ways to think like a 21st century economist which has been translated into 20 languages. Over the past 25 years she has worked with Oxfam, UNDP, and in the Ministry of Trade and Industry of Zanzibar. She currently teaches at Oxford University and Amsterdam University of Applied Sciences.

An introduction with Kate Raworth

Why Doughnut Economics

Kasper: Hi Kate. Being an architect and a developer myself, I see Doughnut Economics as the best way to give a balanced answer to the original Brundtland Commission (1987) definition of economic, social, and environmental sustainability.

What made you conceive the vision of the Doughnut?

Kate: When I studied economics at university back in the 1990s I was deeply frustrated that the implicit goal was economic growth, endlessly – no matter how rich a nation already was – and I refused to accept that the destruction of the living world should be framed as 'an environmental externality.'

Many years later, in 2009, when I first encountered the nine planetary boundaries framework, created by Johan Rockström, Will Steffen and many others, it sent a bolt of adrenaline right through me: here were Earth-system scientists defining an ecological limit to human economic activity: a circular boundary beyond which we collectively should not go. I saw it as the beginning of a new economics, one rooted in respecting and protecting the life-supporting systems of planet Earth.

At the time I was working at Oxfam, where we focused on advocating for people's rights worldwide – such as sufficient food, healthcare, education, living wages, decent work, political voice, and personal security. This made me think: if there is an outer limit beyond which humanity's collective resource use should not go, so too there is an inner limit of human rights, below which no one should fall. So just as there is an ecological ceiling there is a social foundation. I drew a set of social boundaries within the planetary boundaries and in the process turned the circle into a doughnut. The image rapidly gained traction when it was first published in 2012, demonstrating the power of pictures to reshape world views, and also revealing many people's strong desire to recognize and engage with the interconnectedness of the world's social and ecological challenges.

Kasper: My journey of how to define and practice sustainability in urban development started with the 'Cradle to Cradle' philosophy and the regenerative approach of "doing more good" rather than "doing less bad."

Then came the introduction of Circular Economy that focuses on creating man-made ecosystems and business models that could support and scale solutions for a world without waste.

Now, we introduce the Doughnut for Urban Development as a sector-focused manual with frameworks for how to address the ecological ceiling, social foundation, and business design.

Would you agree that Doughnut Economics is a continuation of the above-mentioned thinking, and what do you think it offers additionally?

Kate: The Doughnut aims to provide a compass for the 21st century, but what kind of mindset would enable us to get there?

That's the question I sought to answer in writing Doughnut Economics, and I read widely across disciplines to do so. The book *Cradle to Cradle* by Michael Braungart and Bill McDonough was one of those memorable 'a ha!' moments for me, including its focus on going beyond being '100% less bad' to 'doing good.' In addition, Janine Benyus' work on biomimicry, Herman Daly's foundations of ecological economics, and Dana Meadows' approach to thinking in systems were also huge influences on me.

So yes, Doughnut Economics is a continuation of these ideas, and aims to weave them together so that they dance on the same page. In addition, the Doughnut brings powerful and accessible images and metrics that make these concepts visual and quantifiable at different scales. Doughnut Economics also brings an explicit focus on distributive design alongside regenerative design, focusing on ensuring that value created is shared far more equitably with all who co-create it – and that ultimately turns out to be the whole of society.

Crucially, Doughnut Economics also highlights how today's high-income nations are structurally dependent on endless growth – financially, politically, and socially – and the importance of overcoming that structural dependency. Because right now we have economies that need to grow, whether or not they make us thrive, and what we need are economies that enable us to thrive, whether or not they grow.

Changing Society

Kasper: In my experience the building industry is a business-as-usual industry... In other words, it is an industry that adapts and changes at a very slow pace. In opposition to this, we see rapid changes in other industries ex. the way Tesla currently challenges the car industry and Airbnb disrupts the hospitality industry. More over, we see rapid ideological changes in society within climate change and social structures, for example the 'Fridays for Future' and Occupy Wall Street movements.

It seems evident to me that when younger generations will become decision makers, we will move away from the business-as-usual towards business guided by planetary ethics and societal values.
In your experience, how can the Doughnut challenge and change business-as-usual thinking?

Kate: Instead of starting with the structures of the economy that we have inherited and asking, 'how can we make things a little better?', Doughnut Economics starts with the goal: meeting the needs of all people within the means of the living planet - and from here it asks, what kind of economic thinking and practice will give us even half a chance of getting there?

Over the past few years, the team at Doughnut Economics Action Lab has been working with pioneering practitioners in education, in communities, in business, in urban design, in local government, to create a series of tools and workshops that help to turn the core concepts of Doughnut Economics into entry points for transformative practice.

Through working with these practitioners we have learned how they are beginning to challenge the usual ways of thinking, and therefore how they can start to change the concepts they work with, the processes they follow, and the impacts they have in the world. We've been blown away by the ambition, creativity and generosity of these pioneers and we have learned just how powerful the leadership of their initiatives can be for creating peer-to-peer inspiration that ripples out to inspire others just like themselves. And, yes, younger generations are indeed often at the forefront of these new ways of thinking and doing.

Kasper: Can you share an example of such a change in thinking that is relevant to urban development?

Kate: The need for more, and more affordable, housing is a common challenge in many towns and cities, given growing urban populations and rising costs of living in the face of extortionate rents. And yet, especially in high-income, high resource-using countries, if city policymakers were to adopt the business-as-usual response – constructing more new housing to keep meeting demand – the impact would quickly generate even higher carbon emissions and global material footprints, which need to be falling not rising.

Taking account of both social and planetary boundaries at the same time, in addressing the future of housing, invites questions that lead to a new set of solutions. How can we create more accessible and affordable housing within the housing stock that already exists? How can existing buildings be renovated in a circular, or cradle-to-cradle, way that minimises additional energy required and makes the most of materials already in use? How can these renovations seek to bring back nature's generosity into the city? And how can this renovated housing be owned and governed – for example by the city, or by a community-led housing initiative – in ways that will ensure it remains affordable and accessible for lower-income households that are crowded out of the private rental market? Responding to these questions, and working creativity between both social and planetary boundaries, is the design challenge of our times.

Redesign of Business

Kasper: The dual focus of the Doughnut is indeed unique. We need to both consider the environmental, but not least the social impact of urban development. Our current climate crisis is quite evident to most, but the social implication of urban development remains to be not fully recognised. We are both facing a climate crisis and a housing crisis, and we need to tackle both at the same time, otherwise one will reinforce the other.

However, I would like to end by highlighting a third Doughnut focus that was articulated to me during the making of this Doughnut for Urban Development: the deep design of business. We cannot make radical change in any industry, without a radical redesign of business.

How important is the nature of an enterprise's business model in order to implement Doughnut Economics?

Kate: It's absolutely key. Because ultimately what will shape the future is not the design of individual buildings or products but the design of business itself. At Doughnut Economics Action Lab we take inspiration from the work of Marjorie Kelly and focus on five deep design features, asking: what is your company's purpose in the world? How does it treat its employees, customers, suppliers and allies? How is the company governed? How is it owned? And, ultimately, how is it financed?

These five design features deeply shape what a firm, company, or enterprise can be and do in the world. Whether it will be stuck in extractive and exploitative relations with people and planet, because that is how it has been designed to behave, to drive fast and high returns to its investors. Or whether it can turn to regenerative and distributive practices that can bring humanity into the Doughnut, because it is networked, governed, owned and financed in ways that serve this very purpose.

Kasper: A final question. Are we running out of time, or do you still have hope for people and planet positive urban development?

Kate: Yes of course we are running out of time and I still have hope because there is so much that is necessary to do and still possible to achieve. So let's make it irresistible, and get to work.

"Yes of course we are running out of time and I still have hope because there is so much that is necessary to do and still possible to achieve. So let's make it irresistible, and get to work."

Kate Raworth
Co-founder and Conceptual Lead
Doughnut Economic Action Lab

Table of contents

Glossary

Urban Development
Urban development refers to the process of designing, planning, and constructing cities or urban areas to accommodate community needs. In this book, we mainly consider the construction of residential and mixed-use developments. However, many of the principles and strategies are applicable at the neighbourhood and district levels.

Doughnut Economics
Doughnut Economics is a framework proposed by Kate Raworth which aims to steer civilisation towards the Doughnut of social and planetary boundaries. The inner ring, the social foundation represents the minimum social standards required for human well-being, while the outer ring, ecological ceiling represents the ecological limits of the planet. Between these two rings lies a doughnut-shaped safe and just space for humanity.

Social Foundation
The social foundation takes a departure point from the social and economic UN Sustainable Development Goals, defining the minimum set of social standards and conditions that are considered necessary for human well-being and a dignified life. The social foundation provides the basis for ensuring social equity and distributive economic development.

Ecological Ceiling
The ecological ceiling takes a departure point from the Planetary Boundaries framework, referring to the limits and boundaries of the Earth's ecosystems and natural resources. It represents the maximum levels of human activities that can be sustained without a high risk of triggering significant ecological degradation or exceeding the planet's capacity to regenerate.

Safe and Just Space for Humanity
The safe and just space for humanity is defined as the space between the Doughnut's social foundation and the Doughnut's ecological ceiling, which is served by an economy that is regenerative and distributive by design

Planetary Boundaries
Proposed by Johan Rockström and a group of scientists at Stockholm Resilience Centre, Planetary Boundaries is a conceptual framework which defines nine planetary systems and their respective boundaries from within which humanity can safely maintain a stable and resilient Earth system. Once Planetary Boundary boundaries are transgressed there is an increased risk of unexpected irreversible environmental changes. The planetary boundaries are defined by two core boundaries and processes: climate stability (climate change) and healthy ecosystems (fresh water, pollution, biodiversity loss and land use).

Climate Change
Climate change is one of the nine planetary boundaries. Climate change is the result of long-term shifts in weather patterns and increase in Earth's average surface temperature, due to human activities, primarily the emission of greenhouse gases (GHGs) into the atmosphere.

Climate Stability
Climate stability refers to the maintenance of a relatively constant and predictable climate over a long period. It implies a state where the climate system remains within a safe operating space which allows for healthy ecosystems and human societies to thrive in balance.

Carbon Equivalent
There exist various types of GHGs, and CO_2eq is a shortened form used to express different GHGs in a unified unit. CO_2 has been adopted as the standard unit because it is the most prevalent GHG released through human activities. The CO_2eq value of a GHG can be calculated by multiplying its quantity by its Global Warming Potential (GWP). Throughout this report, the terms "carbon" and "CO_2eq" are used interchangeably, both referring to carbon equivalents.

Biodiversity Loss
In this document we refer to the planetary boundary of biosphere integrity as biodiversity loss – referring to loss of the variety and variability of life on Earth, including all

the different species of plants, animals, micro-organisms, and the ecosystems they inhabit. It encompasses genetic diversity, species diversity, and ecosystem diversity - which play a crucial role in maintaining healthy ecosystems and climate stability.

Healthy Ecosystems
Healthy ecosystems, sometimes referred to as functioning ecosystems, are those that exhibit ecological balance - characterised by biodiverse and abundant species, efficient nutrient cycling, and stable interactions among organisms. Healthy ecosystems provide essential services such as clean air and water, soil fertility, pollination, habitat for diverse species and climate stability.

Regenerative Design
Regenerative design moves away from the degenerative, linear practice of "take, make, use, lose." It is an approach that aims to create resilient systems that actively restore and regenerate the environment. It involves designing processes, products, and systems that "do more good" for ecological health and promote resource efficiency while enhancing social well-being.

Distributive Design
Distributive design moves away from the divisive, centralising practice of concentrating opportunity and value in the hands of a few. It is an approach that focuses on addressing social and economic inequalities through the design of systems, policies, and interventions to distribute resources, opportunities, and benefits far more equitably - with the aim of creating a just and inclusive society.

Allocation
In the context of this book, allocation refers to the process of assigning or distributing a share of specific planetary boundaries down to national, sectoral, and project-level scales, with the aim of ensuring that urban development in a given place, stays within its respective planetary boundary share.

Planetary Sustainability
We define planetary sustainability as a state in which all human socio-economic activity and systems are scaled within biophysical planetary limits.

Supply Chain
The supply chain refers to the interconnected network of entities (both human and not) involved in producing, distributing, and delivering building materials and services locally (on-site) and globally (off-site). Supply chain encompasses all activities from raw material extraction, production, construction, building operations in use, renovation, and end-of-life scenarios, including the social impacts of such activities.

Deep Design
Deep design refers to the purpose of the business, how it operates in networks, how it is governed, how it is owned, and the nature of its relationship with finance. The deep design of business is crucial for the creation and implementation of the transformative, regenerative and distributive actions required to reach the safe and just space for humanity.

Doughnut Economics: a compass to guide urban development

01

In this chapter we introduce Doughnut Economics as a global compass - a set of concepts and tools that can guide urban development.

In this chapter, we introduce the global Doughnut framework, developed by Kate Raworth, which addresses the social challenges and planetary boundaries humanity faces in the 21st century. This visionary framework provides valuable guidance on how to navigate the complexities of endless growth, emphasising the importance of addressing social issues such as inequality, poverty, and access to basic needs while respecting the ecological limits of our planet. By doing so, we can pave the way for a sustainable and inclusive future.

We then introduce the 'Doughnut Principles of Practice,' which offer practical guidelines for effective decision-making and action. These principles encourage us to adopt a holistic perspective, enabling us to think in terms of interconnected systems, promoting fairness and equity in distribution, nurture human well-being, embrace regenerative practices, prioritise overall planetary well-being instead of letting growth be the goal itself, and to employ strategic thinking in our endeavours.

Further applying the Doughnut framework to the realm of urban development, we introduce the 'Doughnut Unrolled' methodology which involves examining the relationship between local aspirations and global responsibilities through four lenses. These lenses provide a framework to analyse and understand how the aspirations of local urban developments can align with the broader global responsibilities of safeguarding the well-being of all people and the health of our living planet. This approach facilitates the practical application of Doughnut Economics in the context of urban development, laying out the foundations for the chapters that follow in this book.

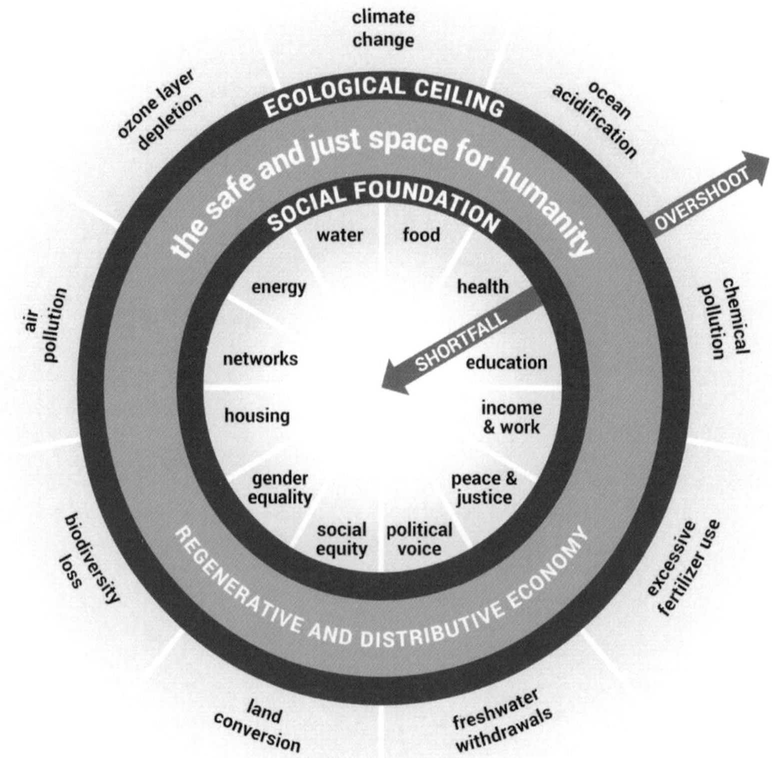

Figure 1: The Doughnut of social and planetary boundaries (Raworth, 2017).

The Doughnut of social and planetary boundaries

The Doughnut of social and planetary boundaries offers a vision of what it means for humanity to thrive in the 21st century - and Doughnut Economics explores the mindset and ways of thinking needed to get us there.

Think of the Doughnut as a compass for human prosperity in the 21st century, with the aim of meeting the needs of all people within the means of the living planet. First published in an Oxfam report by Kate Raworth (2012), the concept of the Doughnut rapidly gained traction internationally, from the Pope and the UN General Assembly to Extinction Rebellion.

The Doughnut consists of two concentric rings: a **social foundation** to ensure that no one falls short on life's essentials (from food and housing to healthcare and political voice), and an **ecological ceiling** ensuring that collectively we do not overshoot our pressure on Earth's life-supporting systems, on which we fundamentally depend - such as a stable climate, fertile soils, healthy ecosystems, and a protective ozone layer.

The Global Doughnut (**Figure 1**) illustrates the ecological ceiling consisting of nine planetary boundaries, as set out by Rockström et al. (2009), beyond which lie unacceptable environmental degradation and potential tipping points in Earth systems. The twelve dimensions of the social foundation is derived from internationally agreed minimum social standards, as identified by the world's governments in the Sustainable Development Goals (United Nations, 2015)

Between the social foundation and the ecological ceiling lies a doughnut-shaped space in which it is possible to meet the needs of all people within the means of the living planet - an ecologically safe and socially just space in which humanity can thrive. However, if humanity's goal is to get into the Doughnut, the challenge is that we are currently far from doing so.

Worldwide, billions of people still cannot meet their most essential needs, yet humanity is collectively overshooting at least six planetary boundaries, and is driving towards climate breakdown and ecological collapse. In **Figure 2** the grey wedges below the social foundation show the proportion of people worldwide currently falling short on life's essentials. The wedges radiating beyond the ecological ceiling shows the current overshoot of planetary boundaries.

The challenge of our times is that we must move within the Doughnut's boundaries from both sides simultaneously, in ways that promote the well-being of all people and the health of the whole planet. Achieving this globally calls for action on many levels, including in the built environment of cities and regions, which are proving to be leaders of driving such change. The Doughnut for Urban Development aims to amplify that potential.

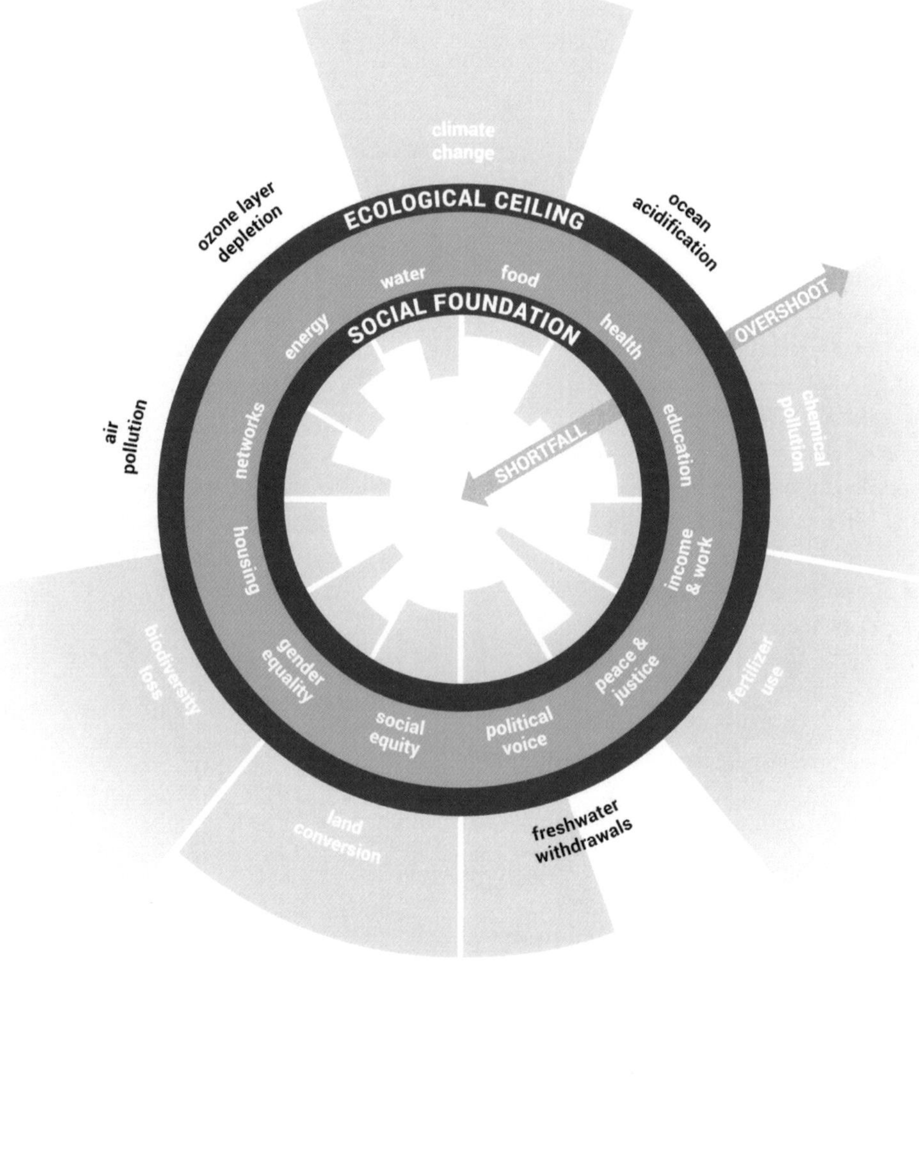

Figure 2: Transgressing both sides of the Doughnut's boundaries (Raworth, 2017) with updated planetary boundaries from 2022.

Doughnut principles of practice

The Doughnut's holistic scope and visual simplicity, coupled with its scientific grounding, has turned it into a convening space for big conversations about re-imagining and remaking the future. Kate Raworth's book (2017), 'Doughnut Economics: seven ways to think like a 21st century economist', further explored the economic thinking needed to bring humanity into the Doughnut, drawing together insights from diverse economic perspectives in a way that everyone can understand. It is now being discussed, debated and put into practice in education and in communities, in business and in government, in towns, cities and nations worldwide.

Doughnut Economics proposes an economic mindset that's fit for our times. It's not a set of policies and institutions, but rather a way of thinking, to bring about the regenerative and distributive dynamics that this century calls for. Drawing on insights from diverse schools of economic thought - including ecological, feminist, institutional, behavioural and complexity economics - it sets out seven ways to think like a 21st century economist to transform economies, local to global.

The starting point of Doughnut Economics is to change the goal from endless GDP growth to thriving in the Doughnut. At the same time, see the big picture by recognising that the economy is embedded within, and dependent upon, society and the living world. Doughnut Economics recognises that human behaviour can be nurtured to be cooperative and caring, just as it can be competitive and individualistic.

It also recognises that economies, societies, and the rest of the living world, are complex, interdependent systems that are best understood through the lens of systems thinking. And it calls for turning today's degenerative economies into regenerative ones, and divisive economies into far more distributive ones. This entails focusing not only on minimising negative aspects, i.e. doing less bad, but also aiming to do more good in any given project. Lastly, Doughnut Economics recognises that growth may be a healthy phase of life, but nothing grows forever: things that succeed do so by growing until it is time to grow up and thrive instead.

To ensure the integrity of these core concepts, Doughnut Economics Action Lab (DEAL) has created the Doughnut principles of practice, as illustrated in **Figure 3**, that should be followed by any initiative that is working to put the ideas of Doughnut Economics into practice.

Embrace the 21st century goal

Aim to meet the needs of all people within the means of the planet. Seek to align your organisation's purpose, networks, governance, ownership, and finance with this goal.

See the big picture

Recognize the potential roles of the household, the commons, the market, and the state – and their many synergies – in transforming economies. Ensure that finance serves the work rather than drives it.

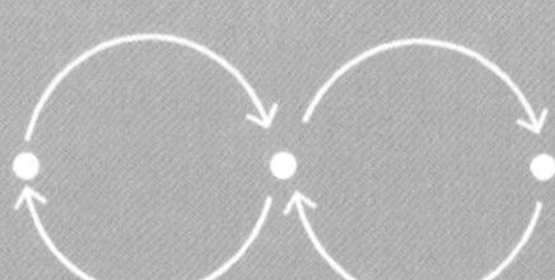

Think in systems

Experiment, learn, adapt, evolve, and aim for continuous improvement. Be alert to dynamic effects, feedback loops and tipping points.

Be distributive

Work in the spirit of open design and share the value created with all who co-created it. Be aware of power and seek to redistribute it to improve equity amongst stakeholders.

Figure 3: The Doughnut principles of practice: Embrace the 21st century goal, See the big picture, think in systems, be distributive, nurture human nature, aim to thrive rather than grow, be regenerative, and be strategic in practice.

Nurture human nature

Promote diversity, participation, collaboration, and reciprocity. Strengthen community networks and work with a spirit of high trust. Care for the wellbeing of the team.

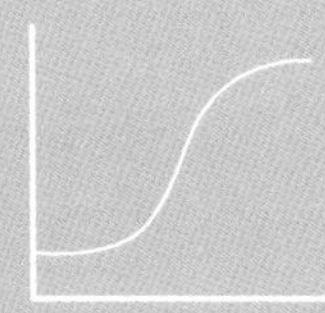

Aim to thrive rather than grow

Don't let growth become a goal in itself. Know when to let the work spread out via others rather than scale up in size.

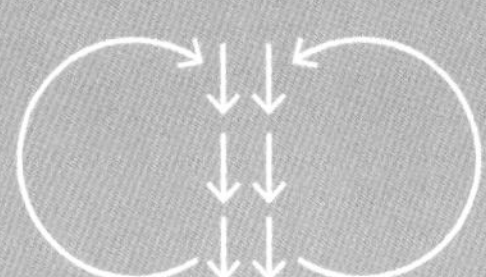

Be regenerative

Aim to work with and within the cycles of the living world. Be a sharer, repairer, regenerator, steward. Reduce travel, minimize flights, be climate and energy smart.

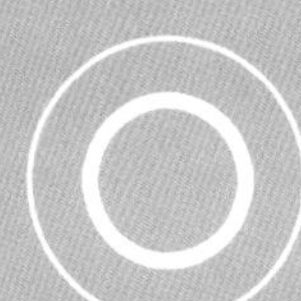

Be strategic in practice

Go where the energy is - but always ask whose voice is left out. Balance openness with integrity, so that the work spreads without capture. Share back learning and innovation to unleash the power of peer-to-peer inspiration.

Introducing the Doughnut for Urban Development

The Doughnut for Urban Development take a departure point in the original Doughnut for social and planetary boundaries. The inner ring, the social foundation represents the minimum social standards require for human well-being, while the outer ring, the ecological ceiling represents the ecological limits of the planet. Between these rings lies the doughnut-shaped safe and just space for humanity that is regenerative and distributive by design.

There are two notable additions. To the social foundation, we have added an additional ring which categorises the 12 original social dimensions by the principles of connected, inclusive, equitable and responsible urban development. To the ecological ceiling, we have added an additional ring which indicates the two core Earth systems of climate stability and healthy ecosystems.

We unroll the social foundation of the Doughnut for Urban Development at the end of Chapter 2 and we unroll the ecological ceiling of the Doughnut for Urban Development at the end of Chapter 3.

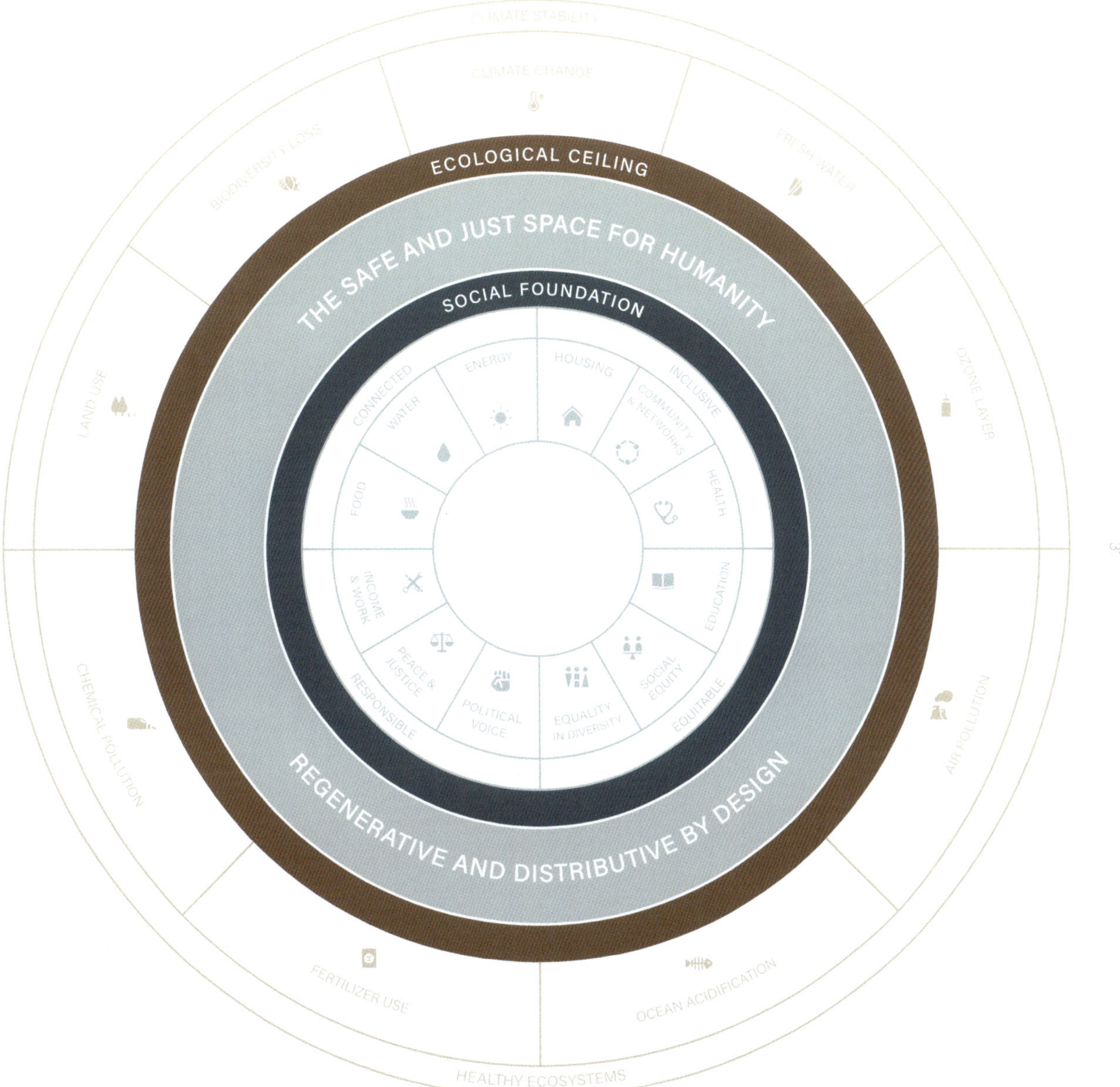

Figure 4: The Doughnut for Urban Development

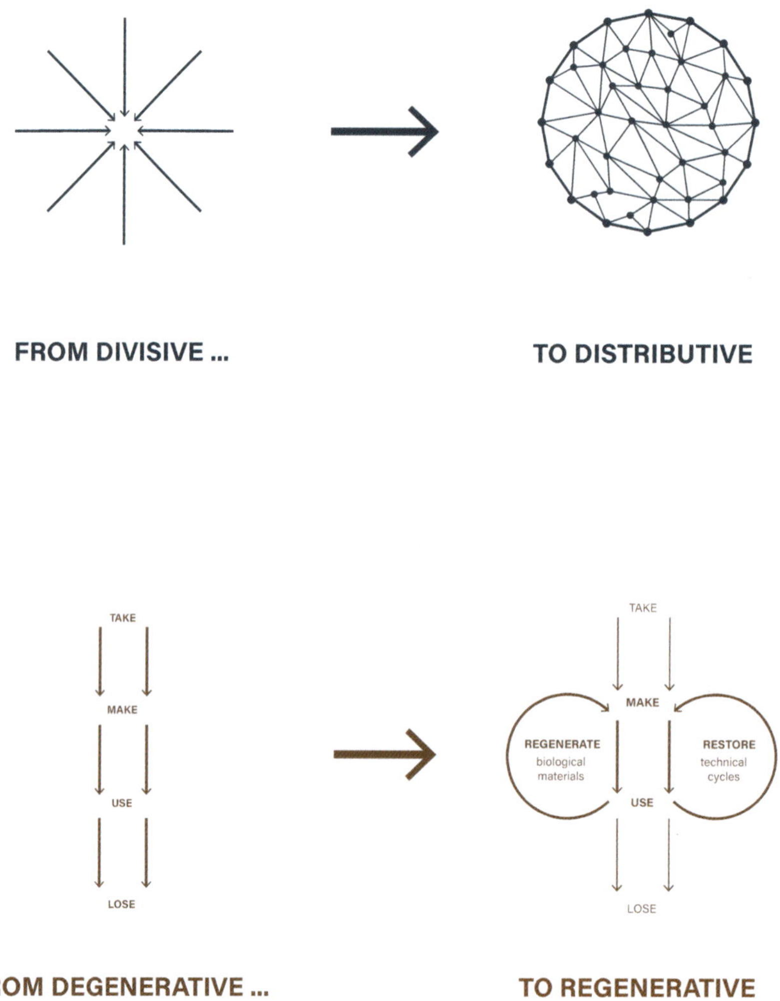

Figure 5: The Doughnut's distributive and regenerative design principles – where we move away from divisive system that drives wealth and opportunity to the hands of the few, towards distributive systems so that value and opportunity are shared more equitably with all who co-create it. At the same time we must move from degenerative, linear processes of "Take, make, use, lose" towards circular, regenerative processes of slow resource use where living systems are regenerated and repaired.

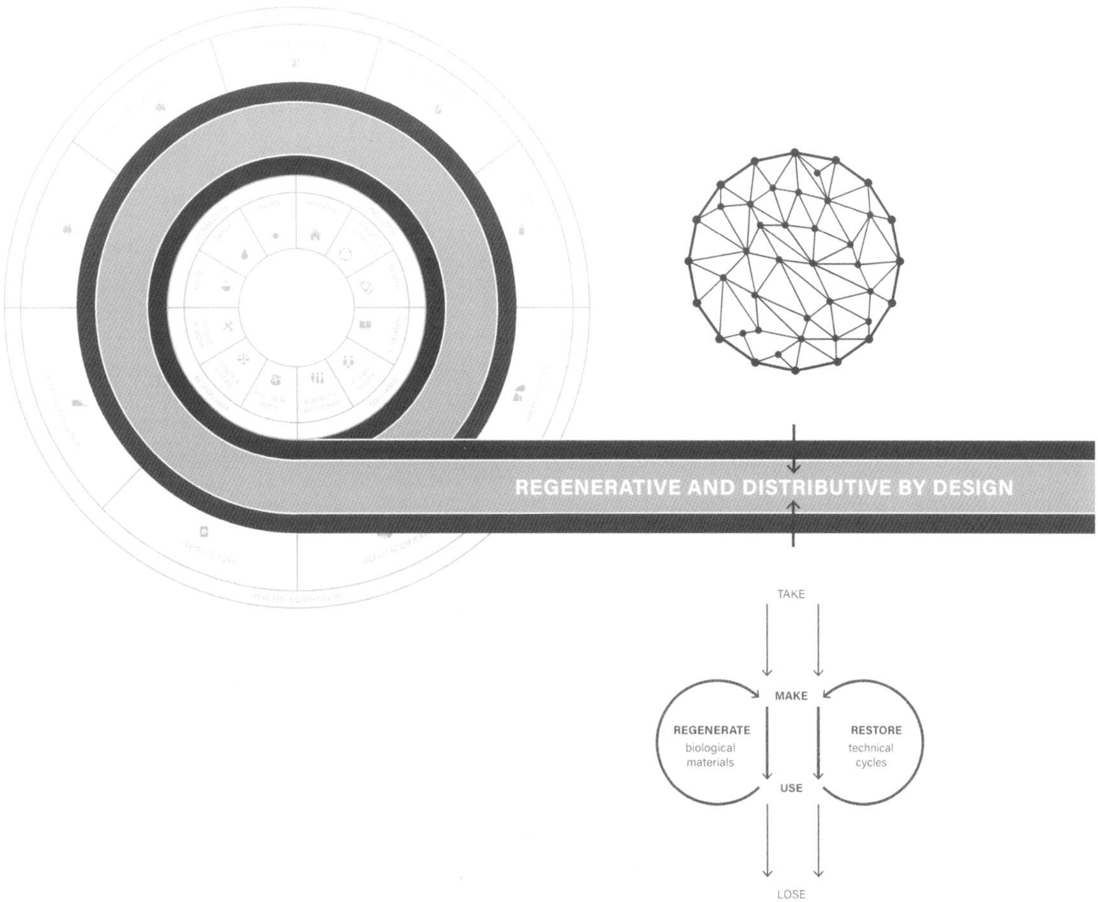

Figure 6: Unrolling the Doughnut to ask: "How can this development bring humanity into the Doughnut through regenerative and distributive principles?" The regenerative design principle shares a relationship with the ecological ceiling, and the distributive design principle shares a relationship with the social foundation.

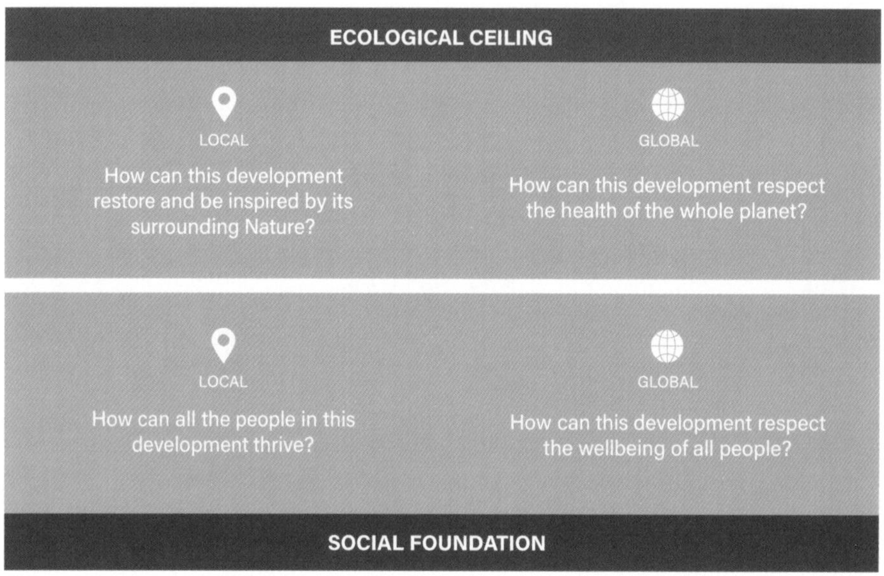

Figure 7: Unrolling the Doughnut into four lenses: local-social, local-ecological, global-ecological, and global-social.

Unrolling the Doughnut: local aspirations, global responsibilities

The Doughnut visualises the goal of meeting the needs of all people within the means of the living planet, but what does this mean for the nations, cities, districts, neighbourhoods or the buildings we live in?

To explore this question in relation to urban development we've applied 'Doughnut Unrolled' (DEAL, 2022), a place-based concept that takes us from the global Doughnut to "four lenses" that invite us to look at the interplay between local aspirations and global responsibilities – both socially and ecologically – to identify possible focus points for transformative action in the buildings we develop and live in
 (**Figure 5-6**).

The four lenses (**Figure 7**) can be used by diverse actors in many ways to practice holistic and interconnected thinking. They are underpinned by the following core questions, framed here for the urban development sector:

The local-social lens asks: how can all the people in this development thrive?
It focuses on identifying the essential elements of a thriving life here, to ensure a basic standard of well-being for all. The local-social lens reflects the lived experience of the residents of a place – recognising the full diversity of their histories, cultures, opportunities and aspirations. Every person has a claim to the essentials that support a thriving life, leaving nobody's voice unheard, and no-one's needs unmet. What "thriving" means will vary from place to place, generation to generation – but every place must transform to make it possible for all.

The local-ecological lens asks: how can this development restore and be inspired by its surrounding Nature?
It focuses on how places can aim to generate as many ecological benefits as their most healthy surrounding natural habitat. The local-ecological lens recognises that every place is situated in a unique habitat, be it a floodplain, a forest, or a desert. If you were to visit the 'wild-land next door' – the healthiest natural habitat in your area – then you would see how nature has learned to survive, thrive and be generous. Nature cleans and cools the air, stores carbon, cycles water, builds nutrient-rich soil, harvests the sun's energy, and welcomes wildlife. What if every place aimed to match or exceed the ecological generosity of its wild-land next door? What would it mean for the design of the places where we live?

The global-ecological lens asks: how can this development respect the health of the whole planet?
It focuses on identifying the many ways that activity and lifestyles here, can impact Earth's life-supporting systems worldwide. The global-ecological lens reveals how every place is connected to the whole planet through the energy it uses, the products it imports and the stream of waste it exports. Think of all the food, clothing, electronics, consumer goods, and construction materials brought daily into your locality, and the stream of waste that flows out. This resource use creates a global footprint that raises humanity's pressure on the planet. How can each place act on its global responsibility to live within planetary boundaries?

The global-social lens asks: how can this development respect the well-being of all people?
It focuses on the many ways that actions taken locally have impacts on people and communities worldwide. The global-social lens explores how actions and decisions taken in every place can have impacts - both positive and negative - in the lives of people worldwide. Global supply chains connect local

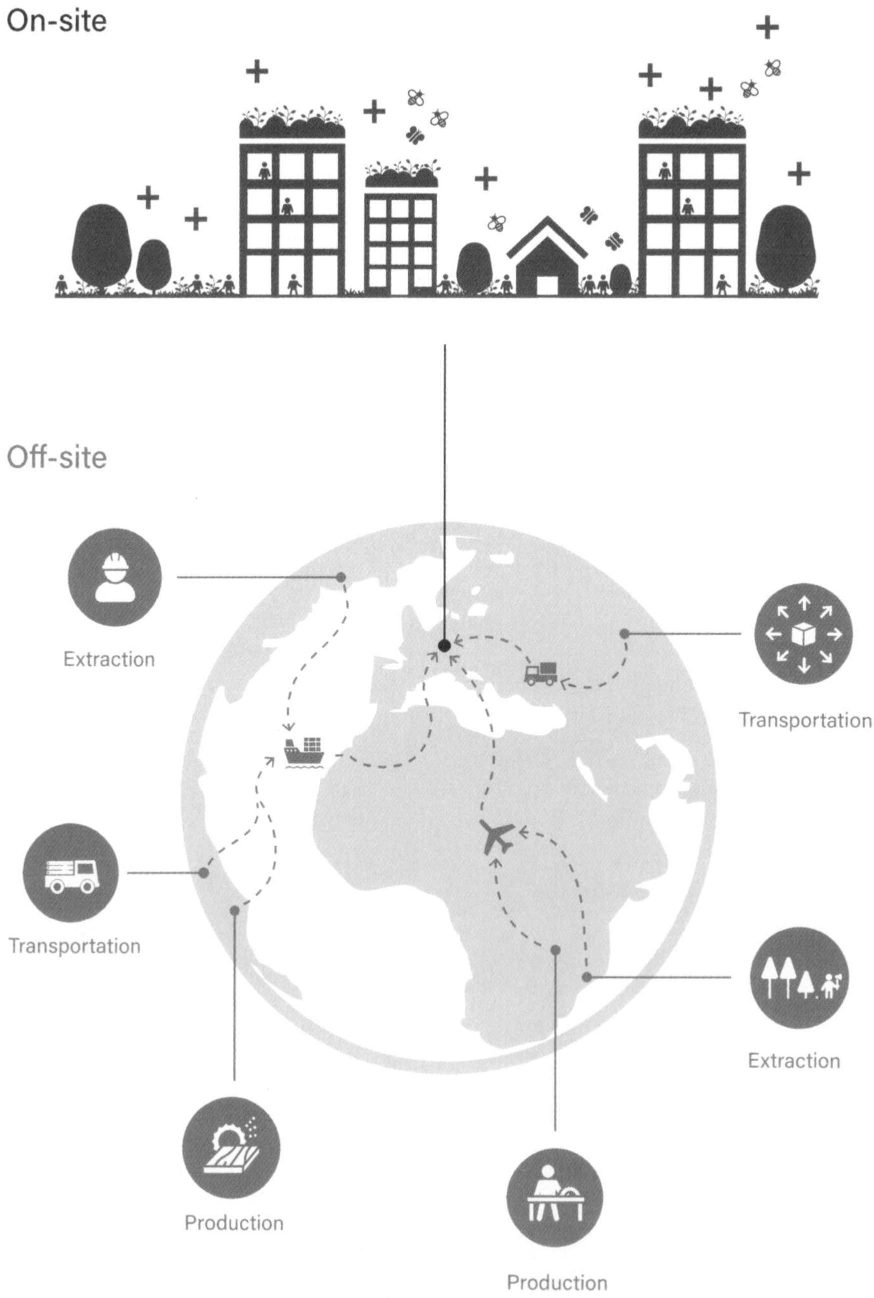

Figure 8: Framing urban development through the local lens (on-site) and global lens (off-site) requires developers to expand the scope of project considerations and face the social and ecological impacts of building construction on faraway places - so that urban development in a European context is not done at the expense of those living across the global supply-chain.

markets to workers worldwide. Cultural connections build solidarity through education, arts and sports. Local policies and attitudes shape how refugees and migrants are perceived and welcomed. In all these ways - and many more - there are opportunities to take action in every locality that help to respect the rights and opportunities of others.

This book focuses on the 'four lenses' to explore a holistic vision of how urban development could help build neighbourhoods and buildings that are homes for thriving people in thriving places, while respecting the well-being of all people and the health of the living planet. The following chapters will elaborate on the initial methodological framework that we have developed, which we are calling: Doughnut for Urban Development.

We introduce the social foundation of the Doughnut for Urban Development in the following chapter.

The 'four lenses' explore a holistic vision of how urban development could help build neighbourhoods and buildings that are homes for thriving people in thriving places, while respecting the well-being of all people and the health of the living planet.

Centrum

The Social Foundation for Urban Development

02

In this chapter we introduce the social foundation for the Doughnut of Urban Development.

First, we outline some of the guiding principles, followed by a review of existing frameworks that we build on top of – such as Sustainable Development Goals (SDGs), Global impact management frameworks, as well as local, regional, and global legislation. The chapter concludes by presenting a comprehensive list of 48 social impact areas to steer urban development towards the safe and just space for humanity.

The 48 impact areas are split across 4 categories: Connected, Inclusive, Equitable and Responsible. For each of the impact areas, we have gathered relevant indicators, tools, and benchmarks in pursuit of practical application for industry actors.

In the appendix, we have gathered:

- Additional methodology references for social impact delivery
- Tools that can be used in the pursuit of social impact
- A library of impact indicators and benchmarks with data sources which make up the Doughnut for Urban Development Database

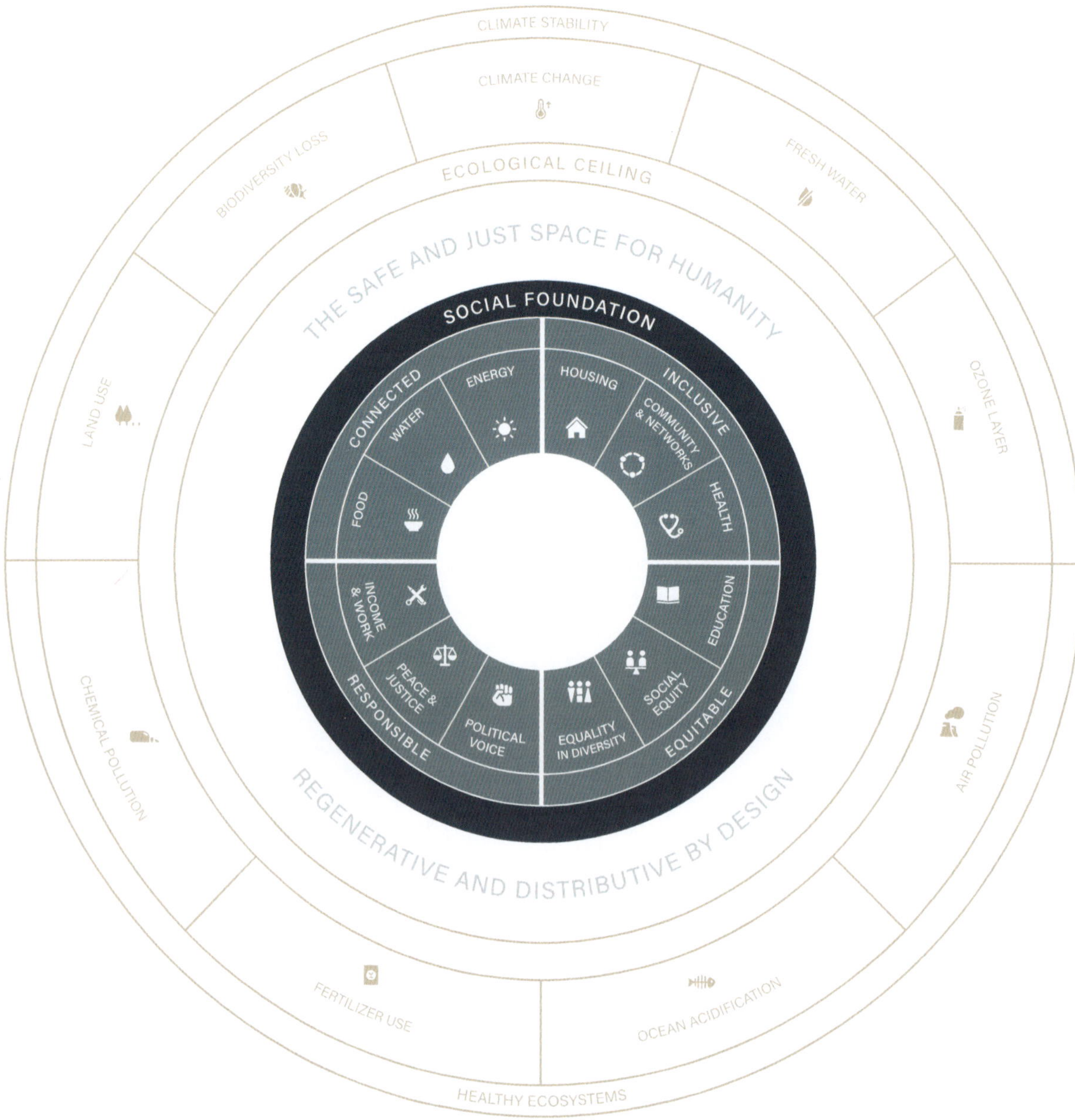

Figure 9: Highlighting the social foundation of the Doughnut for Urban Development

The Social Foundation

The starting point of the Doughnut for Urban Development is the original global Doughnut, which emerges as an increasingly well-researched and widely known foundational framework with clear links to the SDGs. We group the 12 social dimensions of the Doughnut into 4 categories that are useful to consider in an urban development context, namely: Connected, Inclusive, Equitable and Responsible. We describe the rationale for these categories later in the section 'Social Impact Measurement.'

From there, we zoom in on cities, neighbourhoods, local communities, and urban development projects, and identify 48 social impact areas that we believe are important to minimise negative impacts and maximise positive impact across a broad range of social areas, both locally and globally.

The social impact areas cover the full life cycle of urban development projects: from the extraction of raw materials to the acquisition of a land plot; from construction of a building to the operational phase where daily life unfolds; and naturally also considering the end of life for a building.

The importance of holistic thinking: considering global interconnections

In our experience, existing frameworks and methodologies that attempt to monitor social impact are often local in their scope. Few frameworks integrate the significant risks and opportunities for social impacts that take place off-site in the surrounding community and in the global supply chain. As a result the construction sector continues to see poor working conditions, significant safety issues and outright human rights abuses, including modern day slavery.

More locally, our cities are often developed with a strong focus on how to create positive outcomes on each plot, but the surrounding neighbourhood and community are too rarely integrated into the thinking and urban development strategies. This results in positive impact left unrealised and a risk of adverse outcomes because of the isolated, reductionist approach.

With the Doughnut for Urban Development we aim to contribute a holistic framework that can aid actors in urban development to overcome these interconnected challenges and impacts. We have identified 24 global-social impact areas occurring "off-site" that should be included in the scope of urban development projects.

The Health dimension is a good example of the holistic nature – and potential – of the Doughnut for Urban Development as a guiding framework.

Existing frameworks have made important contributions for measuring impacts on the physical health of tenants, with notable frameworks including the German Green Building Council (DGNB) certification scheme, the holistic approach to achieve environmental, social, and governance goals developed by Building Research Establishment Environmental Assessment Methodology (BREEAM), and the International WELL Being Institutes's certification scheme, to name a few. Other more specific tools and frameworks include the VELUX Healthy Homes Barometer (2022) or Realdania's extensive work on indoor climate (2019).

The potential of these frameworks should not be discounted and form an important part of the Doughnut for Urban Development. But none of these frameworks fully succeed in combining key impact areas such as the mental health of tenants, health and safety at the construction site, while also extending these dignities to people working across the global supply chain. The Doughnut for Urban Development aims to start filling this gap, while building on top of existing work.

Maintaining context awareness

We acknowledge that the definition of specific social impacts will be intimately linked to the character, history and context of the community – there is no single "answer" that will be universally correct and completely exhaustive. In this spirit, we invite actors using the Doughnut for Urban Development to view it as a comprehensive starting point for identifying social impact areas, but we similarly stress the need for actors to carefully consider their own unique contexts to assess whether additional impact areas within the 12 dimensions of the Doughnut – and also potential impact areas outside the 12 dimensions – could be needed.

An example illustrating the need for contextual thinking could be an urban development project situated on a plot in an Indigenous community or another marginalised community. While the Doughnut for Urban Development would offer some general impact areas that help the developer navigate key areas concerning such a project, these would need to be contextualised to sufficiently reflect locally relevant cultural, religious, historical or other dimensions that make every community unique.

Although we have attempted to map and list social impact methodologies and tools, and developed an indicator library across all dimensions, we recognise that many other methodologies, tools and indicators exist, and could also be applied when relevant.

In our view, the social foundation of the Doughnut for Urban Development should not be seen as a framework that is fully exhaustive or "finished" – instead, we hope it can serve as a powerful guiding framework and a practical manual that will continuously be further developed and improved by the urban development community.

We acknowledge that the definition of specific social impacts will be intimately linked to the character, history and context of the community – there is no single "answer" that will be universally correct and completely exhaustive. In this spirit, we invite actors using the Doughnut for Urban Development to view it as a comprehensive starting point for identifying social impact areas.

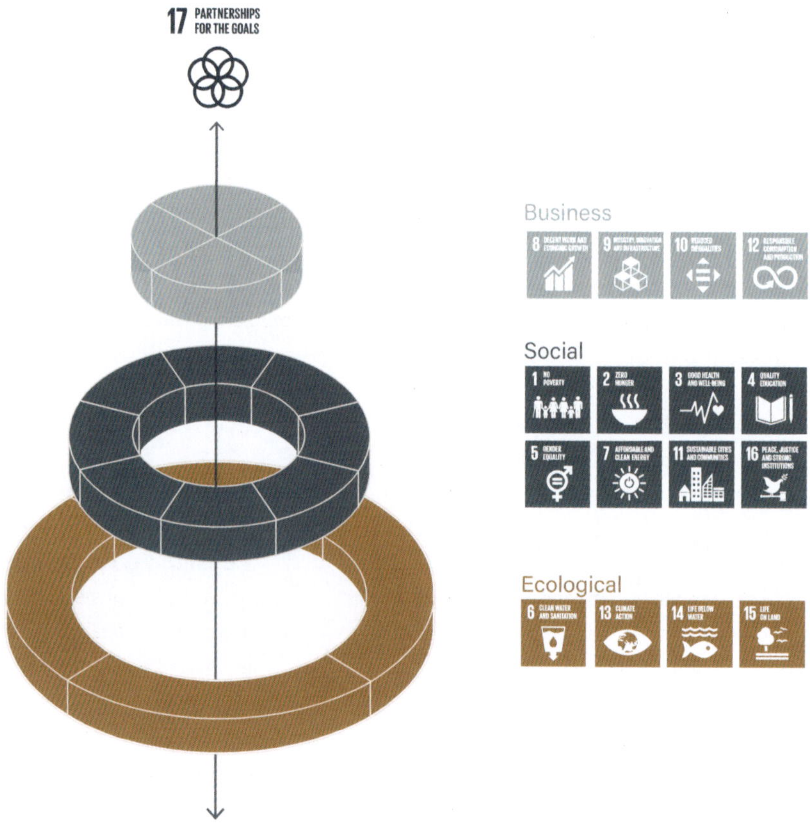

Figure 10: The SDG Wedding Cake was first presented by Stockholm Resilience Institute in 2016 to illustrate how economies and societies should be seen as embedded parts of the biosphere, while underlining the interconnectedness of the SDGs. Without a stable climate and healthy ecosystems, socio-economic goals cannot be achieved, as such we must redesign society (of which the economy is a part) through systems change.

Existing frameworks

The Doughnut for Urban Development is based on a strong foundation of existing impact frameworks to ensure consistency, alignment and the opportunity for benchmarking. Our alignment with existing work strengthens adoption and enables the identification of leaders and laggards when it comes to social impact in urban development.

We have reviewed 850+ impact indicators across 20+ leading impact frameworks in the built environment - from the Global Reporting Initiative (GRI) and the EU Taxonomy to the German Green Building Council (DGNB) and local building codes - and explored how these frameworks are aligned with each other.

Below, we present an overview of some of the existing work and frameworks that we have drawn from and referred to in the development of the Doughnut for Urban Development.

The Sustainable Development Goals
Similar to the original Doughnut, we use the SDGs (**Figure 10**) as a starting point for the social foundation.

The 17 SDGs are powerful for many reasons: they are widely adopted and known across the world, nations have committed to the 169 sub-targets that make up the binding core of the goals, and the goals have been embedded in all parts of society - from the 17 overall goals guiding nation states to UN Global Compact as well as the SDG Action Manager (developed in collaboration with the B Lab) guiding companies to maximise their impact.

The 12 social dimensions of the Doughnut are closely linked to the 17 SDGs and the 169 sub-targets. The Doughnut builds on the SDGs and underlines the needs of humanity (socio-economic SDGs) can only be met if we scale our global operations within planetary limits (Biosphere SDGs).

An important aspect of the SDGs is their focus on the sustainable development of the entire planet, which yields paradoxes in some of the goals: while many countries in the global south are still combating SDG 2 - Ending Hunger, the leading problem in many other countries is not the lack of food but rather severe obesity and excessive food waste. This is reflected by some national adaptations of the SDGs, such as the Danish adaptation from 2020 (Danmark's Statistik & 2030-Panelet, 2020) and has also influenced the link between the SDGs and the Doughnut for Urban Development.

Global impact management frameworks
With the SDGs as the top-level guiding framework, we have gone on to explore some of the leading global impact management frameworks. We have considered the B Impact Assessment developed by B Lab, the Global Reporting Initiative, the IRIS+ framework by the Global Impact Investing Network and the methodology developed by the Impact Management Project among others.

The power of these frameworks is in their wide industry adoption, ensuring that when we present the 48 impact areas of the social foundation of the Doughnut for Urban Development and the accompanying indicator library with benchmarks - the Database - is not completely foreign to industry experts.

Urban development frameworks

The next important level of impact frameworks are the urban development-specific ones. The built environment has some of the most comprehensive impact management frameworks, which guide developers and operators in promoting social and planetary sustainability while maintaining good governance around for example, data transparency and worker rights.

Some of the most widely used frameworks and certification schemes include DGNB, the certification scheme developed by the German Green Building Council, LEED, the certification developed by the U.S. Green Building Council, BREEAM, the certification scheme developed by BRE, and WELL, the certification of the International WELL Being Institute and we have drawn on existing work including the 'Guide to Sustainable Building Certifications' (Jensen et al., 2018) , a comprehensive review of the most widely used certifications schemes.

The advantages of the development-specific frameworks and certifications are their context-specificity, their quantitative data foundations, and their broad adoption enabling benchmarking and comparison. They are – however – limited by their focus on what happens during the construction phase and on the local site, with less focus on the entire project life-cycle and entire supply chain – the global lens of the doughnut.

Local and regional legislation

The final layer of existing work we have considered is the rapidly developing legislative body around urban development. Considering the magnitude of the challenges the built environment is facing today – from the significant impact on our planet to the severe lack of affordable quality housing in cities – it is only natural that lawmakers have identified an opportunity to accelerate a green and just transition.
We surveyed local building codes in the development of the project to draw inspiration and seek benchmarks or indicators that are relevant to the Doughnut. We have, though, refrained from using local indicators in the final overview to ensure that the Doughnut for Urban Development is not limited by national-specific standards, but can be applied at minimum on a European level.

EU Taxonomy

The EU Taxonomy defines a hierarchy for social impact areas, and offers a detailed and legally grounded taxonomy for what it means for an economic activity – such as constructing a building – to be sustainable. It is furthermore closely connected to the flow of capital to urban development (particularly via the Sustainable Finance Disclosure Regulation, 2019) and the reporting and impact management strategies of companies (particularly via the Corporate Sustainability Reporting Directive, 2023).

At the time of writing, the Taxonomy has identified the 'Substantial Contribution' and 'Do No Significant Harm Criteria for two of the six impact areas around planetary sustainability, with the remaining four of the six areas being under development. Similarly, a 'Social Sustainability' taxonomy is under development. Based on the final reports alongside the working group papers published by the EU, the Doughnut for Urban Development is highly aligned with the EU Taxonomy, strengthening its applicability.

Doughnut City Portraits

We have also drawn significant inspiration from the important work done in cities like Amsterdam (Raworth et al., 2020), where 'Doughnut Portraits' at a city-level have been developed. 'The City Portraits' offer a Doughnut perspective placed in between the global/national level and the urban development level, thus provoking us to think beyond local development sites and consider the wider community around urban development projects.

We strongly encourage actors who intend to work with the Doughnut for Urban Development to also explore the 'City Data Portraits' that have been developed and the 'Data Portrait of a Place' tool accessible freely via Doughnut Economics Action Labs website (DEAL, 2023).

Without a stable climate and healthy ecosystems, socio-economic goals cannot be achieved, as such we must redesign society (of which the economy is a part) through systems change.

Defining Social Impact Areas

In this section we discuss social impact and measurement, an impact hierarchy based on EU Taxonomy, limitations to quantifying social impact, and the process by which we defined 24 local and 24 global social foundation impact areas.

Social impact and measurement

In 2050, the UN estimates that 70% of the global population will live in cities. That is an additional 2.5 billion people (UN-Habitat, 2022). This rapid urban population growth has already begun, and it is putting pressure on cities: urban inequality is rising, affordable housing is increasingly scarce and many families are forced to live in conditions of overcrowding or outright unhealthy homes.

It is critical that we meet the challenges of urban population growth with more sustainable and inclusive ways of developing our cities. The aim of the Doughnut for Urban Development is that it can be a central tool in this process, supporting developers in positive societal and ecological impact.

It is not always possible (or even desirable) to quantify social impact. It deals with social relationships, feelings, physical and mental well-being, culture, vibrancy, and much more. What defines a good community, or a good workplace depends on the person you ask and the local context. This requires developers to approach social impact with careful consideration, to avoid the risk of only focusing on measurable matters.

At the same time, we believe that one of the main reasons social impact assessments in urban development are far behind environmental impact assessments is because quantitative social impact management is nascent, making it hard for stakeholders such as investors to formulate specific and ambitious requirements for the social aspects. These social aspects have generally been limited to a handful of social indicators such as indoor climate – which is highly relevant, but insufficient on its own.

Defining a hierarchy

Our proposed way of evaluating if an urban development project lives up to the social foundation is to follow the EU Taxonomy hierarchy of impact. We see the EU Taxonomy (European Commission, 2020) as a new common language for risk and sustainability management across Europe. Furthermore it is anchored in national legislation making it a highly credible and well-researched framework. Therefore, we have used it as a starting point.

The EU Taxonomy defines three levels of impact: 1. Minimum Safeguards (MS): a set of minimum standards that must be fulfilled under areas such as respect for human rights; 2. Do No Significant Harm (DNSH): a set of criteria that must be met for an activity not to create "significant harm", such as a waste recycling threshold to be met and; 3. Substantial Contribution (SC): a criterion that must be met for an activity to have a substantial positive contribution in an impact area compared to the industry average, such as being in the top 15% of energy efficiency.

With The Doughnut for Urban Development, we encourage developers to apply the same logic within each of the social impact areas we define below, though with one important difference: we do not think developers can claim to have a "Substantial Contribution" unless their activity is truly regenerative in practice. This entails having a substantial positive impact rather than simply minimising negative impacts, as illustrated in **Figure 11**. We elaborate on what we mean by "regenerative" in Chapter 4.

Figure 11: Impact levels as defined by the Doughnut for Urban Development: 'Minimum safeguards' and 'Do no significant harm' perpetuate degenerative design , where as 'substantial contributions' are regenerative by design.

In other words, the Doughnut for Urban Development defines three levels of impact:

1. Minimum Safeguards (MS): Is considered as a minimum bar for what is ethically and legally required within an impact area such as respect of local law.

2. Do No Significant Harm (DNSH): is a contribution within an impact area that serves to fully eliminate significant adverse impacts. The activity might still have immaterial adverse impacts, but efforts have been made to manage and reduce material adverse impacts.

3. Substantial Contribution (SC): is a positive contribution within an impact area that is truly regenerative. It does not merely serve to be sustainable, but actively enhances the social outcome that is pursued.

Quantifying social impact

In future work, we hope to be able to add numbers on what it means to reach Minimum Safeguards, Do No Significant Harm and Substantial Contribution within each of the social foundation impact areas. That has, however, not been possible in this edition of this Manual due to time and resource constraints.

The 3-tiered approach should therefore only be seen as a guiding principle to activate project teams when they discuss their positive and adverse impacts across the 48 impact areas and push for regenerative outcomes.

That also means that the Doughnut for Urban Development should not be seen as a certification or a framework that is possible to "comply" with – instead, it should inspire the pursuit of holistic impact assessment and serve as a practical tool.

Introducing the social impact areas

In this section, we introduce the 48 social impact areas in the Doughnut for Urban Development. For each social impact area we considered where an actor has agency to affect change, both locally and globally, drawing on the Doughnut unrolled methodology.

The social foundation lenses are understood in terms of local aspirations and global responsibilities, asking:

The local-social lens: How can all the people in this development thrive?

The global-social lens: How can this development respect the well-being of all people?

An "impact area" should be seen as an area in which an actor in the urban supply chain has a risk of adverse impact or an opportunity to create positive impact, if they approach the area with the right impact management strategies and tools. Under dimensions with wide impact risks and opportunities – such as Health – we have been forced to keep the impact areas more high-level. Under dimensions, where impact risks and opportunities are more limited – such as Energy – we have been able to be more specific in the impact areas.

The 48 impact areas are the product of four integrated work-streams:

1. A translation of the original 12 dimensions of the Doughnut to maintain the link from the global level down to the urban development level.

2. A mapping and analysis of existing frameworks to ensure that we build on top of existing best-practice while making adoption accessible and aligned with ongoing work

3. Three multidisciplinary workshops with a broad group of actors in urban development – from researchers to engineers, architects, developers and human rights experts

4. A Sounding Board process in which our drafts and ideas have been critically examined and further developed to uncover blind spots and nuance our contributions

Collectively, these four work streams draw on a combination of existing best-practice and innovative thinking to push the social impact field towards new territory.

That also means that the Doughnut for Urban Development should not be seen as a certification or a framework that is possible to "comply" with – instead, it should inspire the pursuit of holistic impact assessment and serve as a practical tool.

It is not always possible (or even desirable) to quantify social impact. It deals with social relationships, feelings, physical and mental well-being, culture, vibrancy, and much more.

What defines a good community, or a good workplace depends on the person you ask and the local context. This requires developers to approach social impact with careful consideration, to avoid the risk of only focusing on measurable matters.

The social foundation of the Doughnut for Urban Development

The social foundation of the Doughnut for Urban Development details 24 local and 24 global impact areas across the Doughnut's original 12 dimensions. Alongside the impact areas, we have mapped and listed impact methodologies and tools, and built a 'Doughnut for Urban Development Database', which we hope will enable the industry to advance its social impact strategies and make it easier to put value on and track social impact performance.

In some areas such as Health, the list of tools, indicators and benchmarks found in existing work is long and impossible to fully capture. In other areas such as Food or Political Voice, existing work is limited, and we have been challenged when developing the framework. The impact areas fall under the 12 dimensions of the Doughnut resulting in two local and two global impact areas for each dimension.

In the following pages we unroll the social foundation, to define the impact areas, and give an example of the type of indicator you can use to measure the impact areas. We use building cases to give an example of how you can apply impact areas in practice. None of these cases satisfy each and every one of the 48 impact areas, but all provide tangible evidence of how you can begin integrating Doughnut principles in your next project.

LOCAL / GLOBAL
In order to apply Doughnut principles we must oscillate between designing for social impact locally and social impact globally.

IMPACT AREAS
The 48 impact areas are a direct extension of the 12 dimensions. Each dimension has 2 local and 2 global impact areas.

SOCIAL FOUNDATION
The 12 dimension and 4 categories, together make up the social foundation of the Doughnut for Urban Development.

CATEGORIES
The 12 social dimensions are grouped into 4 categories: Connected, Inclusive, Equitable, and Responsible.

DIMENSIONS
The 12 social dimensions derive for the socio-economic SDGs.

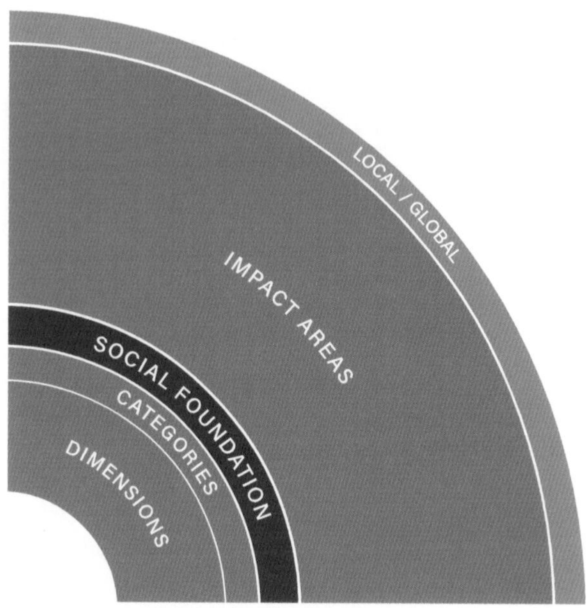

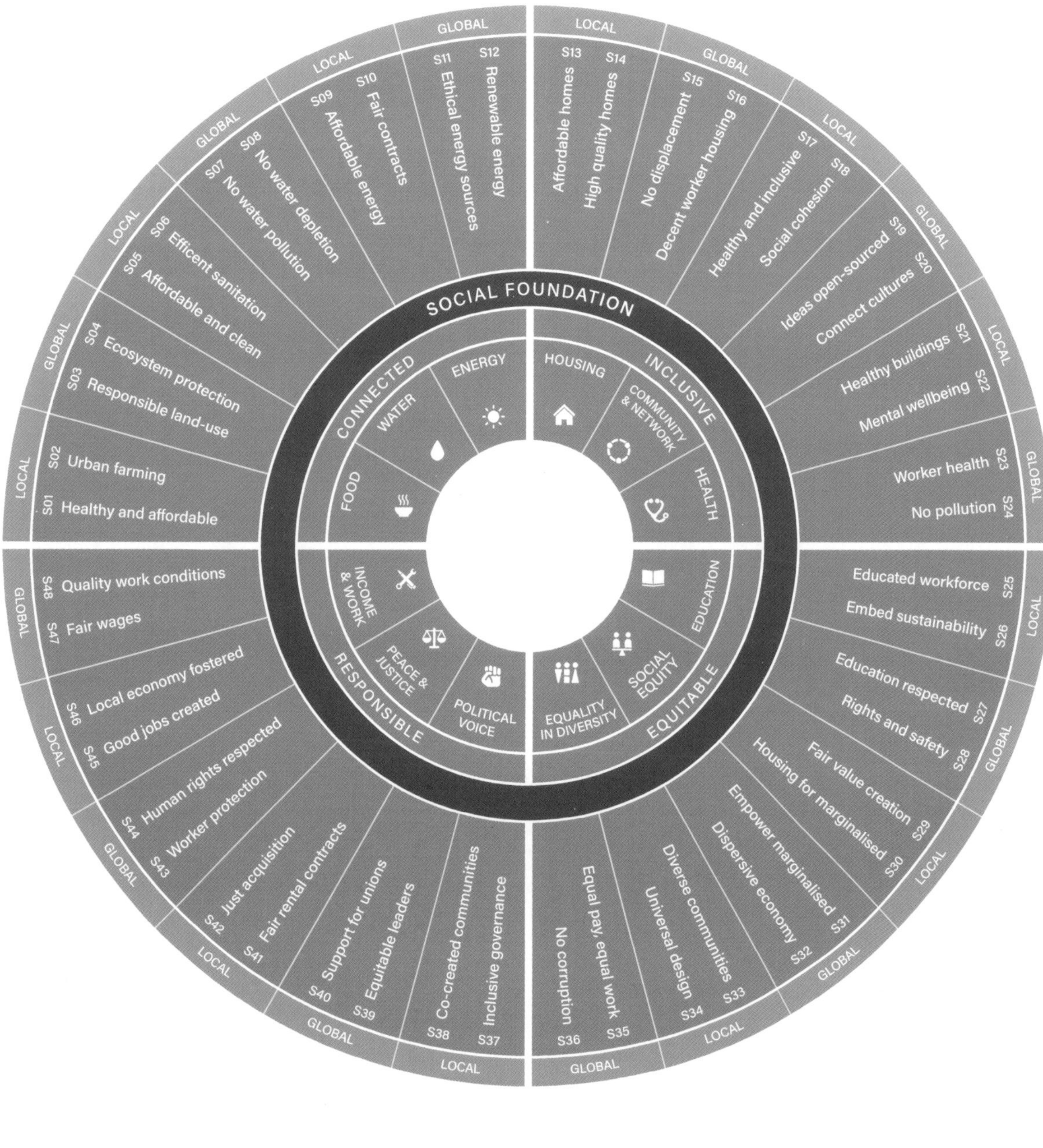

Figure 13: Local and global impacts areas in the social foundation of the Doughnut for Urban Development

SOCIAL FOUNDATION
CONNECTED / LOCAL & GLOBAL

Connected development

Recognising the interconnectedness of urban development and their ecosystems, we must consider areas such as water, food, and energy from a holistic standpoint. By ensuring sustainable access to clean water sources, promoting local and resilient food systems, and transitioning to renewable energy sources, urban development can not only enhance the well-being of their residents, but also contribute to the health of the planet. This interconnected approach between local and global aspirations strengthens the bonds between ecosystems, and the broader global community. The impact areas and example indicators presented here are some of the strategies that can be used to create connected developments.

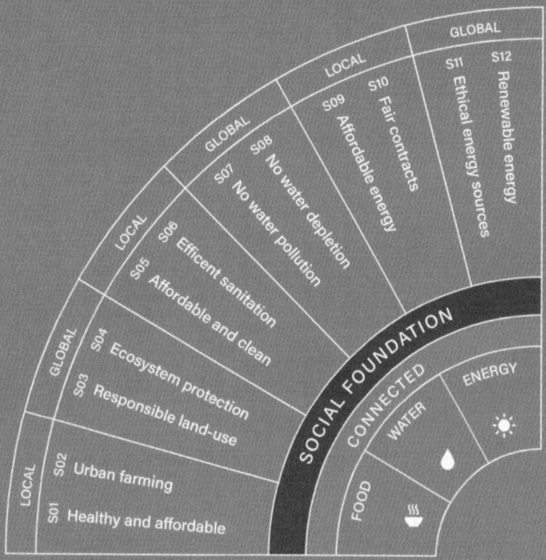

Case Study: Hammarby Sjöstad
Impact Categories: S06, S12

Hammarby Sjöstad exemplifies the concept of "connected" urban development, with a particular focus on specific impact areas. The project prioritises water conservation by striving to halve residents' water consumption through integrated solutions, including wastewater treatment and management of natural water sources. This aligns with the indicator "S06 - Efficient Sanitation". Moreover, the project emphasises energy efficiency and incorporates solar panels, aligning with the indicator "S12 - Renewable Energy". Overall, Hammarby Sjöstad demonstrates a comprehensive approach to sustainable development by addressing key aspects of water conservation and renewable energy.

City: Stockholm. Developer: City of Stockholm. Masterplan: Stockholm City Planning Bureau Architect: Year: 2004 - 2016. Size: 150 ha

FOOD

Local

S01: Healthy and Affordable.
Developments should be near to and/ or provide healthy and affordable supermarkets and other necessary shops for the local community, working to mitigate food deserts and nutrient deficiencies in urban areas.

Example Indicator
Number of healthy and affordable supermarkets and shops within a 10 minute walk

S02: Urban Farming
Local communities should have access to participating in communal urban farming and / or access to purchasing affordable, locally grown produce. Such resources should be distributed in an equitable and just way.

Example Indicator
% of communities with access to urban farming initiatives or local produce

Global

S03: Responsible land-use
Land-use issues involving food production are monitored transparently and avoided. For example, construction materials should not displace or limit access to quality food options within supply chain communities or pollute local environments.

Example Indicator
Number of land-use issues identified and resolved

S04: Ecosystem Protection
Adverse impacts of food production on ecosystems are monitored transparently through adequate risk assessments throughout the supply chain. Adverse impacts on are monitored and eliminated.

Example Indicator
% suppliers screened for significant biodiversity impacts

WATER

Local

S05: Affordable and clean
Access to clean and affordable water is a human right and should be guaranteed to the community.

Example Indicator
% of community with access to affordable & clean water

S06: Efficient sanitation
All sanitation installations are sustainable and efficient, such as "low flow" sinks and toilets. Waste handling is managed in a sustainable way, in which nutrient rich waters are preserved and processed on-site.

Example Indicator
% of community with sustainable & efficient sanitation installations

Global

S07: No water pollution
Water pollution risks, related to the extraction of virgin resources and production of materials are monitored transparently and eliminated throughout the supply chain, including end-of-life scenarios. The creation of materials in faraway places should not leave local water supply polluted.

Example Indicator
% of suppliers implementation water management practices to avoid pollution in supply chain

S08: No water depletion
Water depletion risks, e.g. from virgin material extraction and production of materials are monitored transparently and eliminated throughout the supply chain, including end of life scenarios. The creation of materials in faraway places should not leave the local water supply depleted.

Example Indicator
% of water used that is returned to the environment sustainably

ENERGY

Local

S09: Affordable energy
Local communities should have access to affordable and renewable energy. Urban development should divest from fossil fuels, where alternative energy infrastructure is in place.

Example Indicator
% of community with access to affordable & renewable energy

S10: Fair contracts
Prepayment practices for energy should be transparent and fair to ensure consumer protection, informed decision making around energy usage and expenditure, avoidance of hidden costs, and promote financial inclusion by providing equitable energy services.

Example Indicator
Transparent and fair pre-payment practices

Global

S11: Ethical energy sources
Energy sourcing for building operations and supply chain activities should be ethical and monitored transparently. contributing to sustainable development, climate change mitigation, reduce reliance on fossil fuels, while protecting the environment.

Example Indicator
% of energy from ethical sources in supply chain activities

S12: Renewable energy
Where possible, supply chain activities should support the renewable energy transition. As such, building materials should be sourced from producers who's energy is supplied by renewable energy sources.

Example Indicator
% of renewable energy use in supply chain activities

SOCIAL FOUNDATION
INCLUSIVE / LOCAL & GLOBAL

Inclusive development

Housing, Community & Network, as well as Health, play crucial roles in building inclusive cities. By providing affordable housing options and promoting mixed-income neighbourhoods, urban development can cultivate diverse communities where people from different backgrounds can interact, learn from one another, and build social capital. Supporting community initiatives, fostering social networks, and ensuring healthy and accessible homes, not only benefit local residents but also contributes to the global aspirations of creating inclusive and interconnected societies. The impact areas and example indicators presented here are some of the strategies that can be used to create inclusive developments.

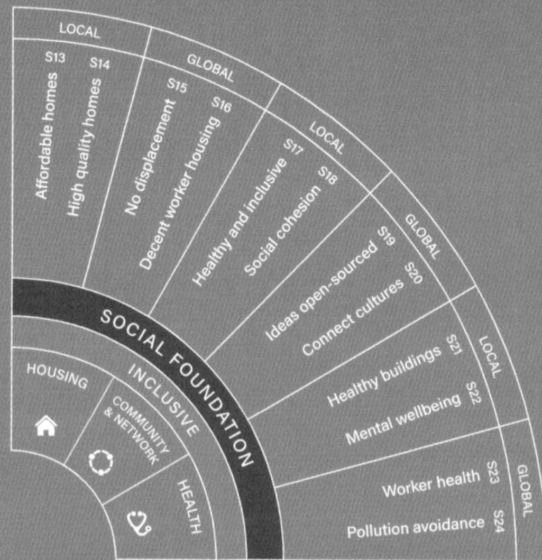

Case Study: The Tingbjerg Houses
Impact Categories: S17, S20

The Tingbjerg Houses serves as a prime example of "inclusive" urban development, placing a strong emphasis on creating inclusive neighbourhoods, as indicated by "S17 - Healthy and inclusive". The project focuses on revitalising the neighbourhood and constructing new homes in an area characterised by vulnerable residents facing challenges such as limited education, low incomes, high crime rates, and unemployment. The vision for The Tingbjerg Houses is to cultivate a diverse and lively community that celebrates diverse cultures, highlighting the indicator "S20 - Connect cultures". Additionally, The Tingbjerg Houses aims to attract residents who actively engage and contribute to shaping the neighbourhood, fostering social cohesion, and promoting inclusiveness.

City: Copenhagen. Developers: NREP, Copenhagen Municipality, fsb, SAB. Architect: Vandkunsten. Landscape: SLA Year: 2022. Size: 39.000 m2

HOUSING

Local

S13: Affordable homes
Housing should be economically accessible and affordable for tenants from all parts of society. As such, developments should reflect the needs and purchasing power of the local society including economically diverse units, such as social housing, affordable housing, student housing, and housing for the elderly.

Example Indicator
% of affordable housing units

S14: High quality homes
The design and construction of housing should be sustainable, healthy and of high material quality. As such, homes should be well-lit, properly ventilated, made of life-supporting, certified building materials, and connect tenants to natural environments and each other.

Example Indicator
Rate of achievement from recognised sustainability or certification standards

Global

S15: No displacement
Supply chain activities should not lead to the displacement of local communities. The housing we create here in a European context should not lead to the displacement of people in faraway places. Issues related to displacement should be monitored and documented transparently.

Example Indicator
Number of displacement incidents

S16: Decent worker housing
Workers across the supply chain should have access to decent, affordable, and stable housing to ensure the mental and physical well-being and a good quality of life while upholding the dignity and respect of supply chain workers.

Example Indicator
% of suppliers with decent worker housing policy

COMMUNITY & NETWORK

Local

S17: Healthy and inclusive
Create healthy and inclusive communities by including communal services and opportunities to participate and integrate socially. Encourage social inclusion by fostering a sense of belonging through the integration of accessible social spaces.

Example Indicator
User engagement in community health and inclusion programmes

S18: Social cohesion
Create social cohesion by providing tenants and other community members access to social infrastructure such as schools, childcare, sports facilities, and community spaces in close proximity to the home.

Example Indicator
% of community with easy access to social infrastructure facilities

Global

S19: Ideas open-sourced
Successful innovation, new knowledge and novel ideas should be shared open source in both local communities and global networks to promote the adoption of just development practices beyond the insular building project.

Example Indicator
Number of open-source projects or collaborations

S20: Connect cultures
Positive contributions are made in local communities where supply chain activities take place, that enhance, protect, and celebrate the local culture.

Example Indicator
Amount of financial and non-financial contributions to communities

HEALTH

Local

S21: Healthy buildings
Design buildings to promote the physical well-being of tenants. As such, building should be well day-lit, designed for thermal comfort throughout the year, designed for maximum natural ventilation, and designed for optimal acoustic transmission levels.

Example Indicator
Indoor climate score measuring e.g. carbon concentration, temperature and humidity

S22: Mental well-being
Design the building to promote the mental well-being of tenants including a feeling of trust and safety, culturally sensitive levels of privacy, and sense of belonging, enabled by design that includes natural and easy surveillance by tenants, strategic positioning of openings and windows, well-lit outdoor spaces, and active ground levels.

Example Indicator
Tenant satisfaction with safety and privacy

Global

S23: Worker health
Occupational health and safety of workers on site and across the supply chain is monitored and documented transparently for workers employed directly and indirectly across the supply chain. Working in healthy and safe environments is a human right that should be respected.

Example Indicator
Number of work-related injuries on site and monitoring of supplier policy

S24: No pollution
Minimise and mitigate through intervention the adverse impacts of environmental, noise, and light pollution on tenants and workers across the supply chain.

Example Indicator
% of suppliers implementing pollution management practices

SOCIAL FOUNDATION
EQUITABLE / LOCAL & GLOBAL

Equitable development

Focusing on education, social equity, and equality in diversity are crucial for addressing the needs of the most marginalised. Urban development must ensure the right to education and advocate for fair worker rights across the supply chain. By dismantling systemic barriers and providing housing for marginalised communities, urban development can play a vital role in fostering a more equitable ecosystem. This interconnected approach drives the pursuit of just and urban development, addressing local and global needs within the sector context. The impact areas and example indicators presented here are some of the strategies that can be used to create equitable developments.

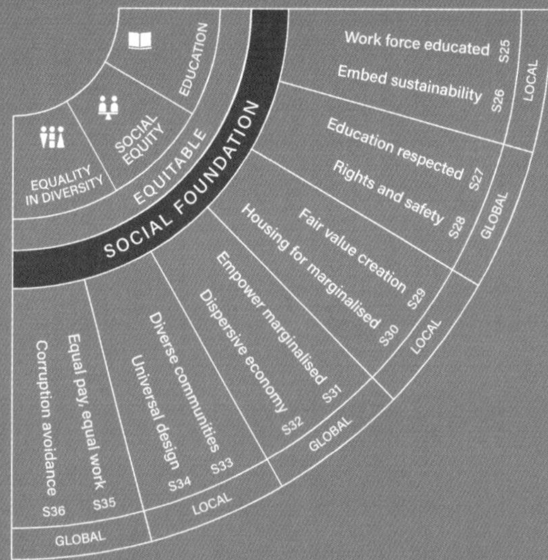

Case Study: Venligbolig Plus
Impact Categories: S30, S33

Venligbolig Plus demonstrates an "equitable" approach to housing development by fostering affordable homes through active relationships. The project focuses on inclusive living arrangements, where two individuals, such as students or refugees, share a living space and provide mutual support. By implementing a mentor or buddy system, pairing students with refugees, the project promotes social responsibility and integration, aligning with indicators like "S33 - Diverse communities" and "S30 - Housing for marginalized". The Venligbolig Plus units, spanning 33 square metres, feature two private rooms, a shared kitchen/living area, bathroom, and terrace. Through the use of compact and innovative spaces, the project aims to provide affordable housing in densely populated areas, while prioritising social considerations and maintaining high-quality housing standards.

City: Frederiksberg. Developers: Frederiksberg Municipality FFB / KAB. Architect: ONV architects, We Do Democracy. Landscape: VEGA. Year: 2017. Size: 2500 m^2

EDUCATION

Local

S25: Educated workforce
The workforce associated with the construction and operation of buildings should be provided education and opportunities for up-skilling within their field, through accessible apprenticeship and traineeships.

Example Indicator
Number of employee training hours

S26: Embed sustainability
Sustainability education is embedded in the design of buildings and spaces e.g. through way-finding. The design should support sustainable behaviour, for example, waste management systems encourage re-use.

Example Indicator
Number of sustainability features incorporated in design

Global

S27: Education respected
The human right to education should be respected throughout the supply chain, to ensure equal opportunities, social and economic development to ensure empowerment and human dignity of workers while working towards inclusive and responsible communities.

Example Indicator
% suppliers screened for educational initiatives and respect for education

S28: Rights and safety
Workers across the supply chain should receive adequate education about their right to occupational health and safety and be educated transparently about the short-term and long-terms risks associated with their field of work.

Example Indicator
% of suppliers with right and safety policy

SOCIAL EQUITY

Local

S29: Fair value creation
Tenants, staff, and other key stakeholders should receive a meaningful share of the value created from the real estate activities concerning them through systems such as rent-sharing agreements, tenant cooperatives or ownership models and long-term lease incentives such as rent stabilisation.

Example Indicator
% of rental income shared with tenants

S30: Housing for marginalised
Developments should provide accessible and affordable quality housing for marginalised groups through the implementation of systems such as inclusive zoning, affordable housing partnerships, subsidised housing programmes, and long-term rent stabilisation.

Example Indicator
% of affordable housing units for marginalised groups

Global

S31: Empowerment of marginalised
Marginalized groups are empowered with rights and protections across the supply chain through inclusive hiring policies, training and capacity building, fair wages and working conditions, and transparent monitoring and reporting of such conditions.

Example Indicator
% suppliers screened for inclusive and empowering activities

S32: Dispersive economy
Value created from real estate activities is dispersed in an equitable way across the supply chain through fair compensation and profit-sharing, direct community initiative support, investment in training programmes, support worker advocacy groups, and transparent and fair bidding processes.

Example Indicator
Distribution of financial value to stakeholders

EQUALITY IN DIVERSITY

Local

S33: Diverse communities
Developers should create and maintain diverse and inclusive communities through inclusive marketing and outreach, culturally sensitive and co-created development, partnership with diverse community organisations, and fair and non-discriminatory tenant selection processes.

Example Indicator
Complience with diversity policy

S34: Universal design
Buildings should be designed after best universal design, accessibility and user-mobility practices, removing physical and environmental barriers, so that all tenants - regardless of age, ability and mobility level thrive at home.

Example Indicator
Compliance with universal design standards

Global

S35: Equal pay, equal work
Equal pay, for equal work is monitored across the supply chain so that all individuals are equaly compensated regardless of sexuality, gender, race, and ethnicity with the aim of creating a more equitable and inclusive society.

Example Indicator
% suppliers compliant with equal pay policy

S36: No corruption
Proper efforts are made to create transparency around and eliminate supply chain corruption, such as conducting thorough due diligence before engaging with material suppliers, create transparent procurement processes, create code of conduct and ethical policies for supply chain stakeholders, and seek third-party certifications and audits.

Example Indicator
% suppliers compliant with anti bribery and corruption policy

SOCIAL FOUNDATION
RESPONSIBLE / LOCAL & GLOBAL

Responsible development

Responsible urban development places community prosperity at the forefront, achieved through citizen empowerment, inclusive governance, and the cultivation of co-created communities. It embraces principles of fair contracts, human rights, and fosters job growth, local economic vitality, and equitable wages. This comprehensive approach extends beyond the mentioned examples, emphasising the interconnected prosperity of communities at local and global levels throughout the real estate supply chain. It specifically addresses crucial areas of social advancement, such as promoting political voice, peace & justice, and ensuring income & work opportunities. The impact areas and example indicators presented here are some of the strategies that can be used to create responsible developments.

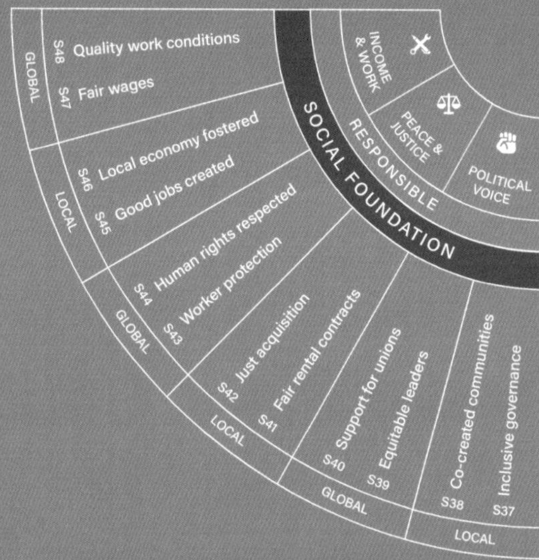

Case Study: Circl Pavillion

Impact Categories: S38, S45

The Circl Pavilion in Amsterdam Zuid is built to foster communities and bridge public and private space, and it is one of the first fully circular building projects in the Netherlands. It has a very strong social intent and exemplifies "responsible" urban development by creating meaningful employment opportunities, aligned with indicator "S45 - Good jobs". It fosters a co-created community, as seen in the employment of speechless staff in the café, in line with "S38 - Co-created communities". Through its welcoming space for collaboration, events, and cultural activities, Circl promotes engagement and interaction, contributing to a sustainable and vibrant urban ecosystem.

City: Amsterdam. Developer: ABN AMBRO. Architect: de Achitekten Cie, Landscape: Donkergroen. Year: 2017 Size: 3.350 m2

POLITICAL VOICE

Local

S37: Inclusive governance
Tenants and other stakeholders are empowered by and included in housing governance by way of board seats, voting rights, and transparent communication of policy matters concerning them.

Example Indicator
% of stakeholder representation on governance body

S38: Co-created communities
Relevant stakeholders such as tenants are given opportunities for co-creating and influencing their community through participatory decision-making processes, creation of social and cultural events, access to shared spaces and amenities, access to skill sharing / support networks and effective communication platforms.

Example Indicator
Number of co-creation initiatives

Global

S39: Equitable leaders
Building industry activity across the supply chain promotes and fosters equitable and non-discriminatory leadership and power structures.

Example Indicator
Representation of leadership diversity (gender, ethnicity, culture, age, education and more)

S40: Support for unions
Building industry activity across the supply chain promotes and fosters equitable and non-discriminatory leadership and power structures.

Example Indicator
% of workforce in unions

PEACE & JUSTICE

Local

S41: Fair rental contracts
Contracts between tenants and landlords are based on fair and transparent terms, and clearly define the responsibilities of and obligations of both parties, notice periods, provisions for dispute resolution, fair policies regarding security deposits and tenant privacy rights.

Example Indicator
Share of tenants on fair rental contracts

S42: Just acquisition
Acquisition and procurement processes related to the development of urban areas, such as acquisition of land, property evaluation, purchase agreements, closing, contract management and post-acquisition evaluations are just, ethical and transparent.

Example Indicator
% of suppliers assessed for ethical procurement

Global

S43: Worker protection
Workers across the supply chain are granted fundamental human rights and protections of those rights. Developers should not engage directly or indirectly with organisations that benefit from forced labour.

Example Indicator
% suppliers screened for respect of human rights and anti-slavery

S44: Human rights respected
Basic human rights such as such as education, health, water and sanitation, gender equality, decent work, housing, food, clean energy, and peace are monitored transparently and respected across the supply chain.

Example Indicator
Number of human rights breaches

INCOME & WORK

Local

S45: Good jobs created
Urban developments must evaluate the need for mixed-use programming to foster local economic activity - such as commercial units for small businesses, co-working facilities, cultural and creative activity, and public community services.

Example Indicator
% of workforce employed from local community

S46: Local economy fostered
Urban developments should include mixed-use programming to foster local economic activity - such as commercial units for small businesses, co-working facilities, cultural and creative activity, and public community services.

Example Indicator
Amount of space for commercial, co-working and other facilities

Global

S47: Fair wages
Equitable and fair wages should be secured for both employees and workers throughout the supply chain.

Example Indicator
% workers in supply chain paid above minimum wage

S48: Quality work conditions
Working conditions for workers across the supply chain should be of high quality, safe, and support well-being. Such conditions should be monitored and reported on transparently.

Example Indicator
% of suppliers assessed for labour practices

The Ecological Ceiling for Urban Development

03

In this chapter we introduce the Planetary Boundaries framework that is the starting point for the ecological ceiling for the Doughnut for Urban Development.

The chapter introduces how human activities, such as urban development, impact the planet's climate stability and ecosystem health, and describes how urban development contributes to transgressing all nine, interconnected planetary boundaries. The chapter concludes with a comprehensive list of 48 impact areas to align urban development with the safe and just space for humanity.

The 48 impact areas are organised by two 2 categories: climate stability and healthy ecosystems. Each impact area consists of actionable indicators, tools and benchmarks ready to be implemented in future development projects.

In the appendix, we have gathered:

- Full description of planetary boundaries control variables
- Tools and methodology for assessing planetary impact including complementary control variables.
- A library of impact indicators and benchmarks with data sources which make up the 'Doughnut for Urban Development Database'.

Climate stability is dependent on healthy ecosystems, and healthy ecosystems are dependent on climate stability.

Currently, these ecosystems are under the threat of losing their collective capacity of regulating the global temperature.
This is why the Earth-system is marching towards an uncertain and risky future.

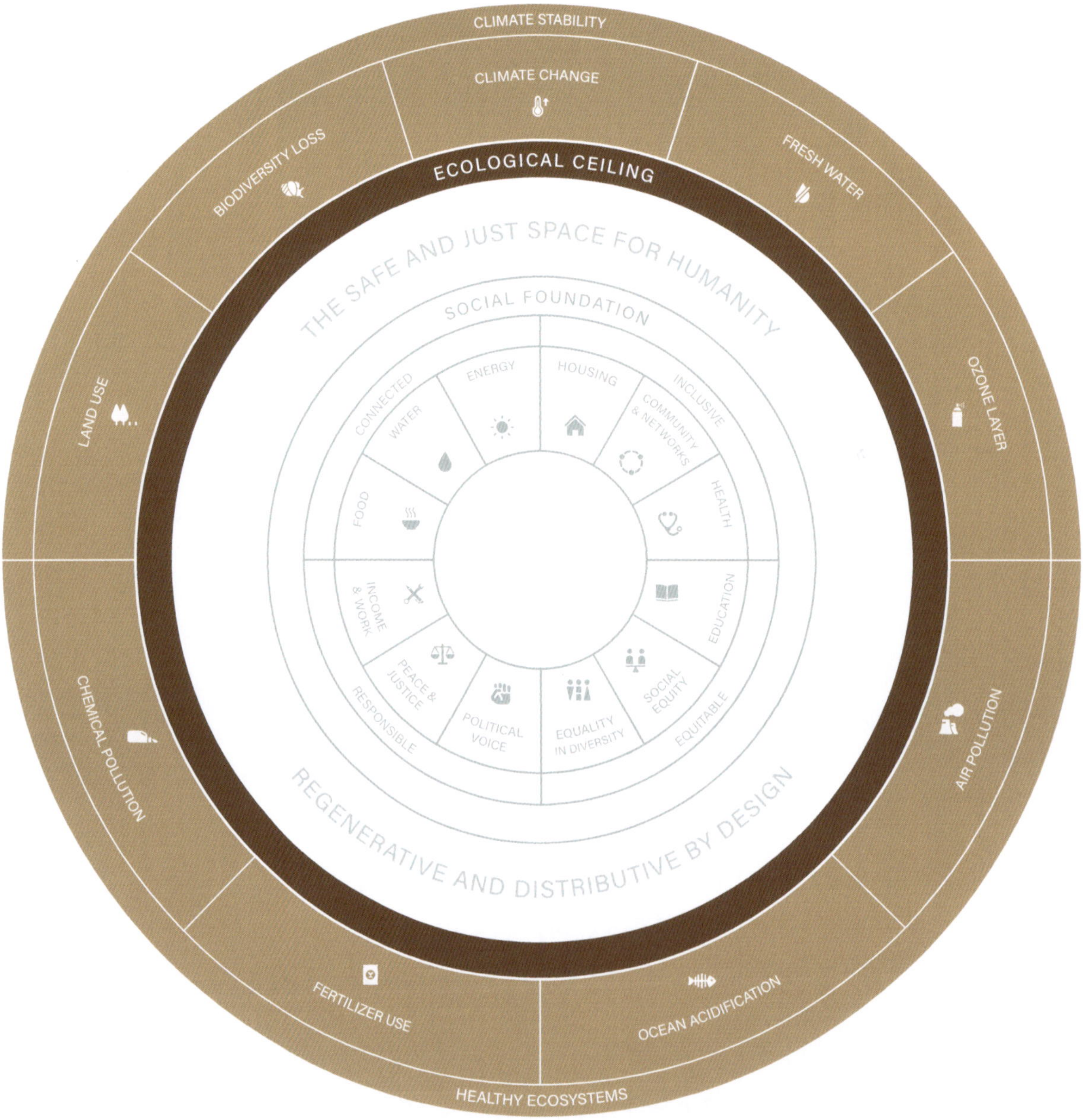

Figure 13: Highlighting the ecological ceiling of the Doughnut for Urban Development

The Earth system is on the move

The history of humanity is a remarkable story of innovation and change. Our journey of what we consider home is evidence of that innovation. Our homes have transformed from a patch in a forest, to a fixed cave in a mountain or a portable tent, to round stone walls of a broach or a rectangle of a dwelling, and to a spacious house in a town or a small apartment in a mega-city. The ability of humans to understand the laws of nature and to transform nature's limited resources led to the rise of cities.

Most importantly, in the same period nature blessed us with an unassuming 11,000 years of stable climate - the Holocene or a Goldilocks state - that is not too hot, not too cold. During this time, reliable seasons emerged, and global air temperature did not change more than 1°C. Looking back in time, we know that such climate stability is an exception rather than the rule, as show in Figure 14. (Dansgaard et al., 1993; Petit et al., 1999, Rockström et al., 2009).

Thanks to these unique circumstances, people could develop agriculture, grow in numbers, settle in more and more places, learn to process materials and eventually build homes and cities, as we know them. Along the way, we discovered global warming caused by a sharp increase in human-led carbon emissions, carbon concentration, and global air temperature, at a rate beyond what Earth has ever seen.

We also discovered that the mechanism of keeping this global, ecological, self-regulating thermostat running is governed by functioning ecosystems, such as Amazonian and Boreal forests and ice sheets at the Southern and Northern poles, and their interactions. Climate stability is dependent on healthy ecosystems, and healthy ecosystems are dependent on climate stability. Currently, these ecosystems are under the threat of losing their collective capacity of regulating the global temperature. This is why the Earth system is marching towards an uncertain and risky future on a hot and unpredictable planet, all while knowing that human activity is the dominant driver, as illustrated in Figure 15.

A major human-led driver is how we build homes and live in cities. History requires us to rise to the occasion and continue our story of innovation. Yet again, transforming what we call home and how we build them - but this time, by doing so, moving the needle in the opposite direction, away from impairing climate stability and degrading quality of ecosystems by dumping greenhouse gases into the atmosphere, and move towards a more stable, healthy future with a thriving and resilient Earth system.

A major human-led driver is how we build homes and live in cities. History requires us to rise to the occasion and continue our story of innovation.

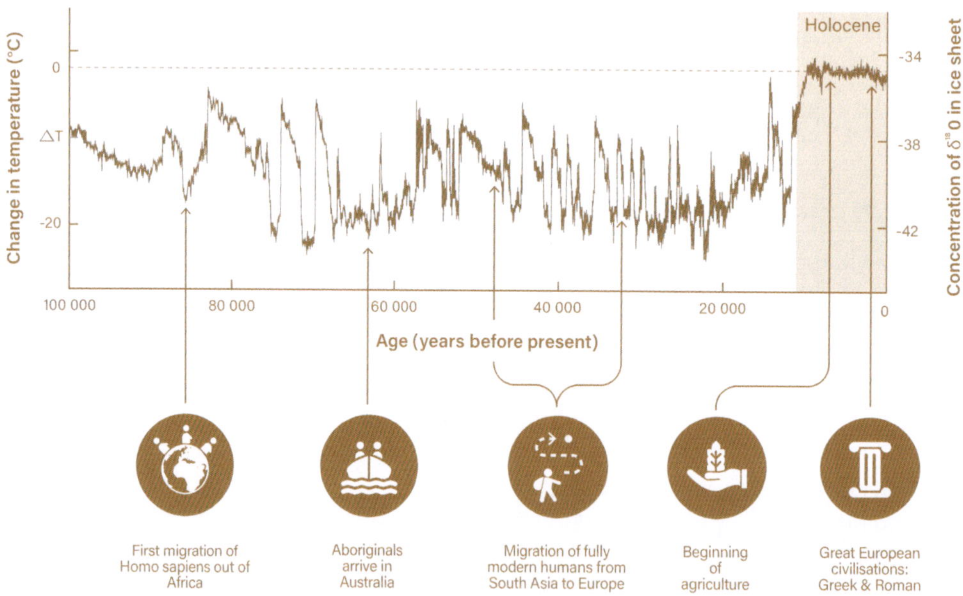

Figure 14: 100,000 years of global temperature, highlighting the Holocene or 'Goldilocks state' and a selection of significant human activities.

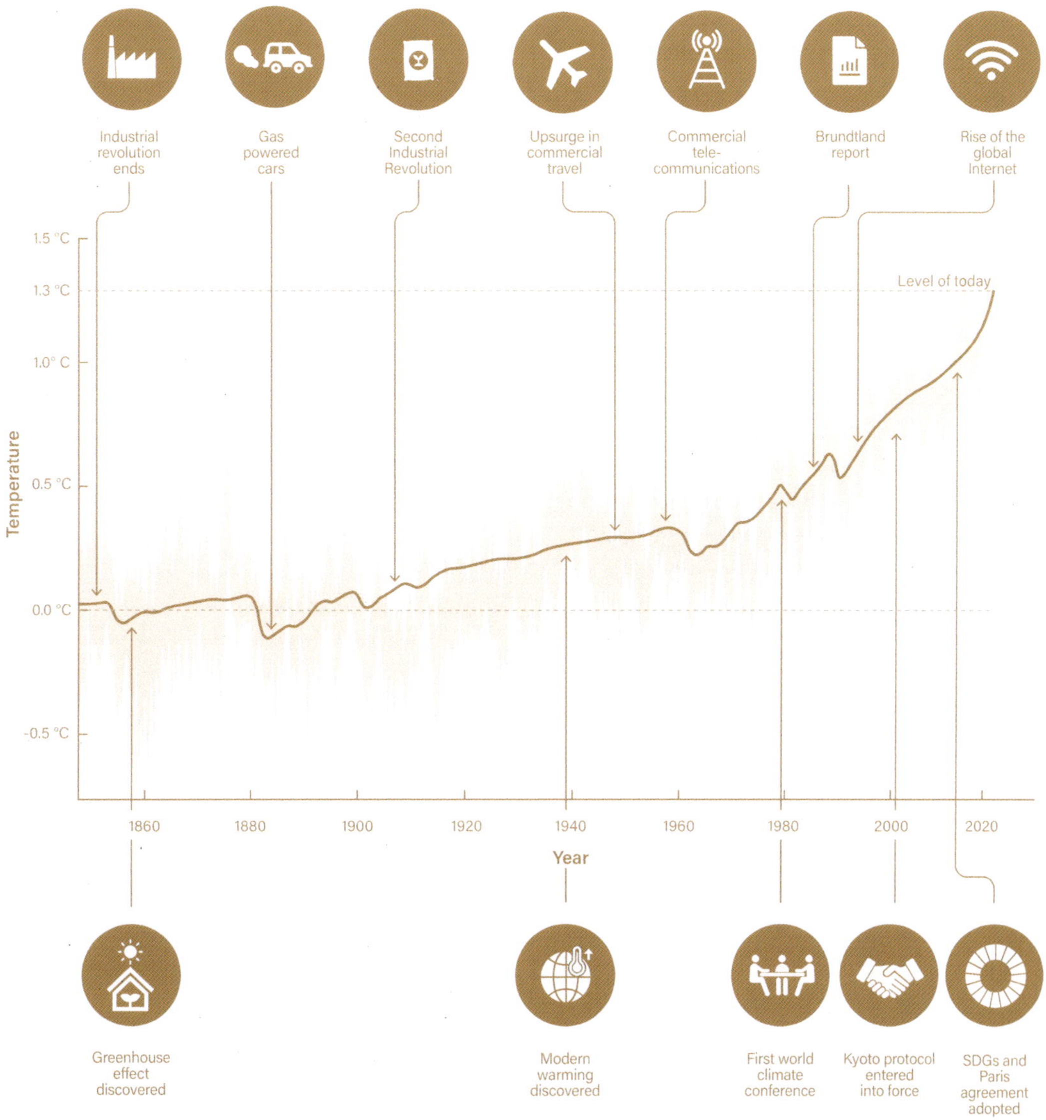

Figure 15: Global temperature from 1800 to present, highlighting a selection of significant human activities.

Figure 16: The planetary boundaries framework tracks human impact on nine essential Earth-system processes at a global scale (Steffen et al., 2015; Wang-Erlandsson et; al., 2022; Persson et al., 2022),. The Planetary Boundaries is a useful framework for understanding human impact on Earth systems and portrays the boundaries as fixed and separate – a tidy snapshot of Earth systems.

The Planetary Boundaries as a guide

Scientists have developed the 'Planetary Boundaries' framework to guide us on this new journey (Steffen et al., 2015). The framework defines a safe operating space for humanity based on biophysical processes that are fundamental to maintaining the stability of the Earth system in a Holocene-like state. As illustrated in Figure 16, the framework includes nine interdependent and interconnected biophysical systems and processes that are modified by human actions, including urban development.

Climate change and **biodiversity loss** are core boundaries because once substantially transgressed, they are able independently drive the Earth system into a new state – away from the Holocene. The other seven planetary boundaries are **ocean acidification**, **land-system change**, **freshwater change**, **stratospheric ozone depletion**, **atmospheric aerosol loading**, **novel entities**, and **biogeochemical flows** (nitrogen, phosphorus pollution), which when transgressed they lead to deterioration in Earth's ability to function, which can increase the risk of regional regime shifts and predispose transgression of the core boundaries.

Where possible, each planetary boundary is associated with one or more measurable control variables that need to remain below a certain threshold to avoid abrupt or harmful changes (Steffen et al., 2015). Such control variables are detailed in the Appendix Chapter 2. Thresholds in six of the nine planetary boundaries have been already transgressed and we are moving rapidly towards increasing risk of planetary tipping points.

Urban development has its share in the transgression of these planetary boundaries. For example, in the EU, the construction sector accounts for 40% of all extracted materials, 40% of energy consumption, generates 40% of waste annually, and contributes to 33% of all greenhouse gas emissions (Sizirici et al., 2021). With all that carries a significant impact on global climate stability and biodiversity loss as well as chemical flows in global supply chains. The urgency is not only in minimising the impact of urban development, to reduce ecological pressures to a well-functioning planet. The following section describes how urban development contributes to the transgression of planetary boundaries.

Linking planetary boundaries to urban development

The construction of a new building impacts all planetary boundaries through different pathways and to different degrees. This complexity originates not least from a diversity of building materials and their unique sourcing and processing. Such impacts can be captured by the Life Cycle Assessment (LCA), as detailed in the following chapter. Nonetheless, there are always choices to be made that will greatly help or hinder our journey towards a safe and just space for humanity, but we're running out of time to course correct.

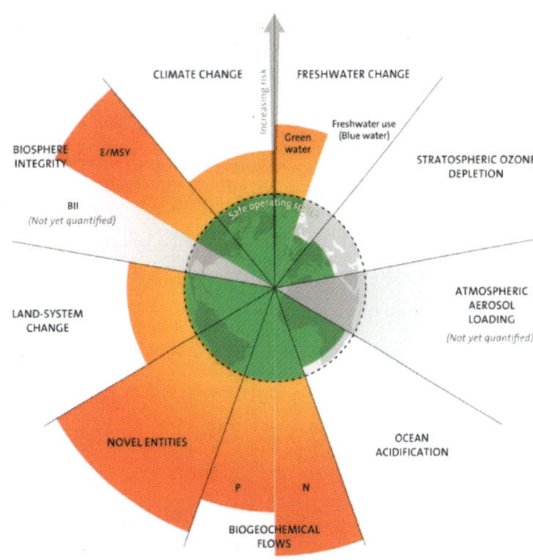

Figure 17: The original Planetary Boundaries framework defined by the Stockholm Resilience Centre, updated in April 2022 (Steffen et al., 2015; Wang-Erlandsson et; al., 2022; Persson et al., 2022).

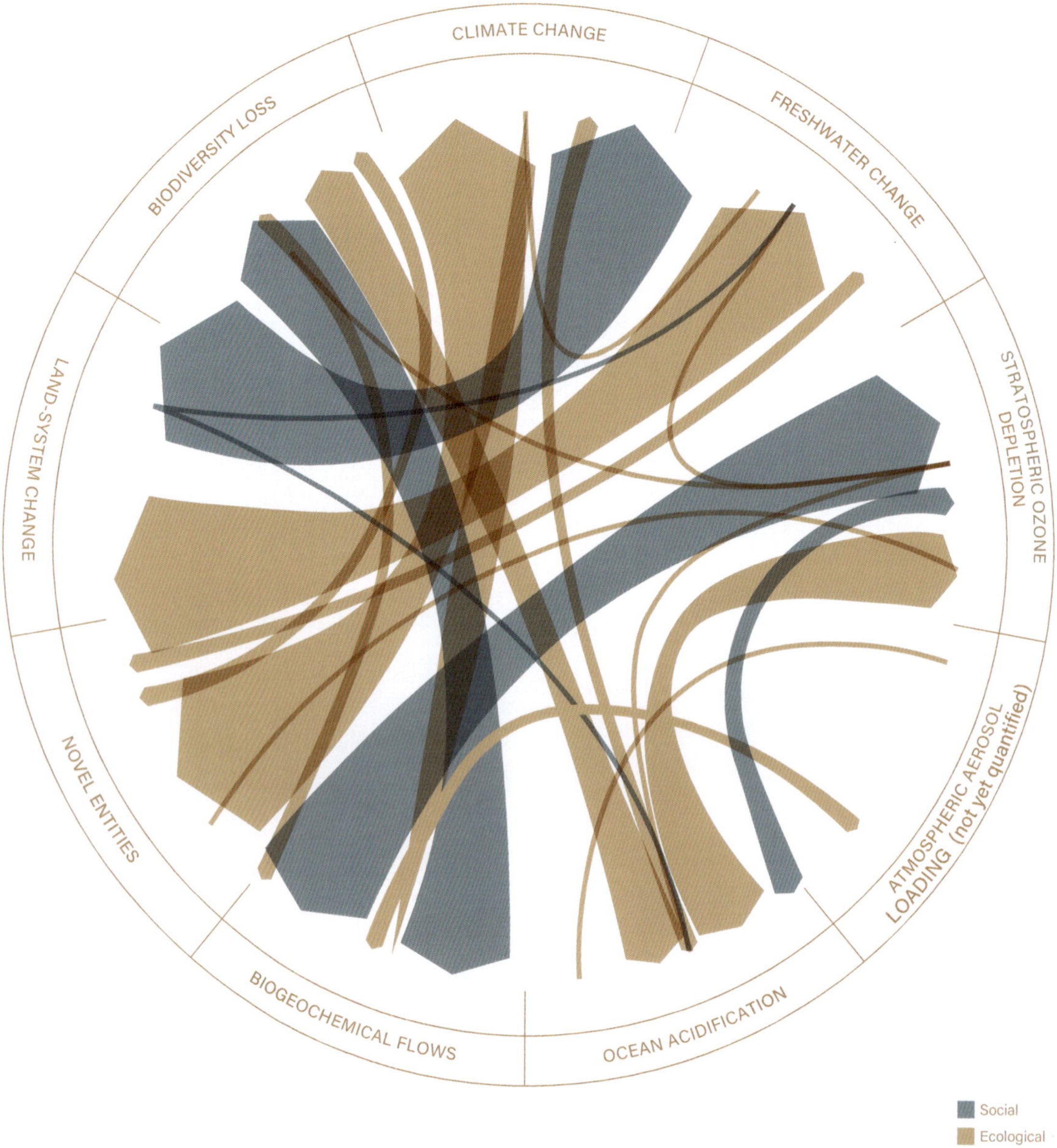

Figure 18: Although planetary boundaries are often conceptualised and measured separately, Earth system processes are complex and deeply interconnected (Lade, S.J., Steffen, W., de Vries, W. et al., 2020).

There are two essential dimensions to developing urban areas within the planetary boundaries. On one hand, we must adopt practices that not only reduce and eliminate the pressure on each planetary boundary, but also reverse these trends. These include avoiding demolition by retrofitting, sourcing materials and products differently than in the past (renting, reusing, or up-cycling) and choosing materials that can store carbon, increase biodiversity, and occupy less land.

On the other hand, we must be able to assess the environmental impacts and benefits of these measures along the entire supply chain and life cycle of a building. This entails setting and assessing environmental performance targets linked with the planetary boundaries. These practices are highlighted briefly here and detailed at the end of this chapter in the ecological ceiling of the Doughnut for Urban Development.

Planetary boundaries: safeguarding climate stability and healthy ecosystems.

The **climate change** boundary defines the composition of the atmosphere that supports life, halts global warming, reduces risks and preserves climate stability. To achieve that, the atmosphere should not contain more than 0.035% (350 ppm) of carbon (Steffen et al., 2019). Currently in 2023, 0.041% (412 ppm) of carbon floats in the air we breathe, basks in the sun to absorb its energy, raising global air temperature and leading to devastating consequences which include more frequent and more severe droughts, prolonged heat waves, intense flooding, powerful hurricanes, rising sea levels and more **acidic oceans.**

Oceans absorb roughly 25% of human emissions and in the process are becoming more acidic which is detrimental for marine biodiversity and their ability to regulate the climate by absorbing less carbon. The planetary boundary of **ocean acidification** will remain within the safe space if the climate change boundary is respected.

No matter the location, every local emission contributes to the global rise of carbon levels. Therefore, to develop urban areas within the climate-change planetary boundary it is critical to know the accumulated carbon contribution from the entire supply chain and the life cycle of a building, which currently is too high. Life Cycle Assessment (LCA) is a well-established method capable of estimating carbon footprint and used as an indicator for the most impactful reduction interventions. The use of LCA in relation to planetary sustainability is introduced further in Chapter 4. Actions informed by LCA could include moving away from heavy emitting materials towards low carbon, local solutions.

The other three boundaries concerning the composition of the atmosphere are **ozone depletion**, **aerosol loading**, and **novel entities.**

Ozone-depleting substances such as chlorofluorocarbons (CFCs) and hydro-chlorofluorocarbons (HCFCs) have been banned in the European Union under the Montreal Protocol (United Nations, 1987). Since the ban, the ozone layer is on its way to recovery. Although ozone depletion does not require immediate action from the construction sector, this is a powerful reminder of a success story which should be repeated for other harmful substances such as carbon, plastics, small particles and novel entities.

Aerosol loading, defined as the number of small particles suspended in the air, which impacts the functioning of the Earth system in many ways (Stocker et al., 2013) and leads to about 7 million premature deaths per year (World Health Organisation, 2022). Fossil fuel combustion, diesel transportation, fossil-

Figure 19: The planetary boundaries include two core Earth systems climate stability and healthy ecosystems, which impact the state of Earth systems and are impacted by rapidly rising anthropogenic pressures. This figure is adapted with permission from an original concept by Sarah Cornell, Tiina Häyhä and Holger Hoff (unpublished work).

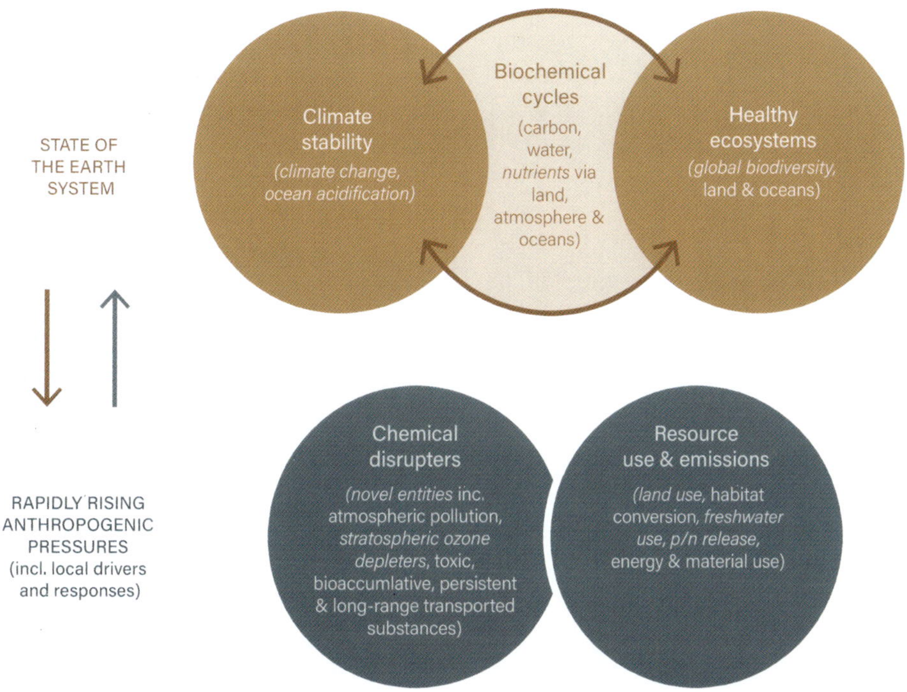
STATE OF THE EARTH SYSTEM
Climate stability
(climate change, ocean acidification)
Biochemical cycles
(carbon, water, nutrients via land, atmosphere & oceans)
Healthy ecosystems
(global biodiversity, land & oceans)
RAPIDLY RISING ANTHROPOGENIC PRESSURES
(incl. local drivers and responses)
Chemical disrupters
(novel entities inc. atmospheric pollution, stratospheric ozone depleters, toxic, bioaccumlative, persistent & long-range transported substances)
Resource use & emissions
(land use, habitat conversion, freshwater use, p/n release, energy & material use)

based energy generation, cooking and heating with biofuels generate small particles by emitting sulphates, nitrates, black carbon and organic carbon. This is where the construction sector can make a difference by electrifying cooking appliances and transportation, avoiding demolition, implementing dust control measures for example wetting surfaces and covering materials, using fossil-free energy, promoting cycling and the use of public transportation, all with the aim to keep air quality high, in line with European and international health standards. There are several EU regulations and directives that regulate aerosol loading from construction projects which can serve as a reference such as, the Industrial Emissions Directive No 2010/75/EU or The Construction Products Regulation (CPR) (EU) No 305/2011).

Novel entities are man-made substances and chemicals that pose great threats to a well-functioning Earth system, human health and biodiversity (Villarrubia-Gómez et al., 2018). They accumulate locally and spread globally through air, water and food chain. With time, ecosystems and food products absorb dangerously high concentrations of toxic pollutants leading to contaminated water supplies and soils and decline in wildlife, such as the bee populations (Persson et al., 2022). This is evident in the production of metals such as steel, which relies on pollutants in mining, extraction and refining processes. There are many other building materials from vinyl flooring to flame retardants, spray foam insulation, and lead paints that are inherently toxic for both people and the planet (Denchak, M., 2018).

Currently, novel entities continue to be released into the biosphere at alarmingly high rates and only a fraction of them has been assessed for risk or safety (Persson et al., 2022). Therefore, it is critical for the construction sector to use alternative low-toxic materials, reduce the use of plastics, and fully contain pollutants along the entire supply chain. Cleaner choices are enabled by constantly growing databases (European Union, 2006) and a range of increasingly holistic certification schemes such as DGNB, LEED and BREEAM. Clean alternatives might include nature-derived materials like mycelium, offering a versatile spectrum of products that can replace polystyrene, composite materials and insulation (Wilson, 2011).

Climate stability relies on a global network of well-functioning local ecosystems such as lakes, forests, grasslands and coasts. **Biodiversity loss** is a core boundary that represents the collection of many local ecosystems, their functioning and genetic diversity. Ecosystems function well when they support life - a healthy biological community of organisms, plants and animals in their physical environment. To safeguard biodiversity loss, urban development must halt the loss of natural habitat, slow down the extinction rate, maintain sufficient forest cover (i.e. **land-system change**), use sustainable levels of **freshwater**, and avoid disruption to **nutrient cycles** (i.e. **nitrogen (N)** and **phosphorus (P)**).

Ecosystems operate within local and regional boundaries. Therefore, locations of urban sprawl, off-site sourcing and processing of raw materials, and on-site constructions are key for assessing and avoiding the multiple and context-specific impacts of urban development on biodiversity loss.

In this quest, urban development has a choice to move away from destroying, degrading, polluting, and fragmenting natural habitat and biodiversity, and instead choose to design for clean outdoor air, regenerate healthy ecosystems through the implementation of ambitious nature-based solutions. To keep biodiversity within the planetary boundaries, biodiversity intactness index of habitats needs to be maintained above 90% (Scholes & Biggs, 2005).

Due to resource intensiveness, the construction sector poses the risk of over-exploitation of natural resources such as timber, sand and **freshwater.**

The planetary boundary of **land-system change** aims to maintain 75% of forested land cover which is contested by logging industry and demand for timber. Therefore, the goal is to harvest natural resources slower than they can reproduce. In this regard, biogenic materials such as hemp, present a rapidly renewable alternative. The planetary boundaries also indicate safe levels of withdrawal of freshwater from lakes and groundwater that should not exceed 25-55% of mean monthly river flow during low-flow months (Steffen et al., 2015).

Urban development also alters the flow of life-giving nutrients – **nitrogen (N)** and **phosphorus (P)**. **Nitrogen** is a building block of proteins and **phosphorus** of cell membranes and bones. They are used as fertilisers in urban landscaping to enhance the growth of urban nature – trees, shrubs and flowers. However, when overused, nutrients runoff from soils and concentrate excessively in water bodies, leading to dead zones and eutrophication. Nutrient pollution from sewage discharge, fossil fuel combustion and soil run-off are important impact actions which urban development can tackle with wastewater treatment and recycling facilities, permeable pavements, nature-based solutions such as rain gardens and bioswales and access to ecosystems such as wetlands and coastal habitats.

Complementary indicators related to climate change and healthy ecosystems include human appropriation of net primary production (HANPP) (Haberl et al., 2007; Krausmann et al., 2013), and CAPRO (carbon productivity) (Stoknes & Rockström, 2018) while a complementary analysis can be found in the "Designing for Planetary Boundary Cities" report (Arup, 2021).

Climate stability relies on a global network of well-functioning local ecosystems such as lakes, forests, grasslands and coasts.

Defining ecological ceiling impact areas

This section presents strategies for moving the urban development sector towards regenerative practice to restore climate stability and healthy ecosystems. We bundled these strategies into 48 ecological impact areas.

For each ecological impact areas, we considered where an actor has agency to affect change, both locally and globally, drawing on the 'Doughnut Unrolled' methodology.

The ecological lenses are understood in terms of local aspirations and global responsibilities, asking:

The local-ecological lens: How can this development restore and be inspired by its surrounding Nature?

The global-ecological lens: How can this development respect the health of the whole planet?

Ecological impact areas aim to collectively cover the full life cycle, one step at a time, losing no sight of off-site impacts. This includes the acquisition of a land plot, extraction of raw materials, manufacturing of products, construction, operational and end of life phases. Indicators, tools, and benchmarks associated with these impact areas can be found in the 'Doughnut for Urban Development Database.'

The ecological impact areas are mapped onto the broad categories of climate stability and healthy ecosystems, which underpin the dynamics of the Holocene-like Earth system. This approach implicitly accounts for the fact that all nine planetary boundaries interact with each other. Refraining from rigid categorisation stems from the fact that all nine planetary boundaries interact with each other, and many planetary impact areas can be associated with several different boundaries simultaneously (**Figure 18** and **Figure 19**).

Identifying Ecological Ceiling Impacts Areas

The selection of the Ecological Ceiling Impacts Areas was developed through three integrated work streams:

- "Down-scaling" and translating the planetary boundaries from global level to urban development scale using allocation principles and Life Cycle Assessment, as detailed in Chapter 4.

- Mapping and analysis of existing frameworks and best practices such as SDGs, global impact management frameworks, urban development specific frameworks such as DGNB, LEED and BREEAM, and Biodiversity Net Gain - local and regional legislation, and Doughnut Economic Action Lab's 'Data Portrait of a Place' tool.

- Three multidisciplinary workshops with a broad group of actors in urban development, involving researchers, engineers, architects, developers, ecologists and human rights experts.

Through such a process, the Doughnut for Urban Development aims to provide a holistic guide that reflects the planetary impacts of urban development and their complex interconnections. We invite the wider urban development community to join us in co-creating future iterations of the Doughnut for Urban Development framework together, following the open-source philosophy, by adding new tools, indicators, methods, benchmarks, and sharing examples of best practices. We wish for the framework to evolve with time and reflect the needs of the planet and the diversity of its residents.

Organising impact areas by climate stability and healthy ecosystems

Climate Stability

Climate stability is threatened by the high concentration of carbon and other greenhouse gases in the atmosphere. Every local emission, no matter how small, leads to global consequences. Every one of them counts because carbon accumulates and remains in the atmosphere for a long time, between 300 and 1000 years (Buis, 2019).

Currently, urban development is responsible for an unsustainable, large amount of carbon emissions that are distributed along the entire supply chain and across the lifespan of a building. These phases include the choice of raw materials, its extraction and processing, transportation, construction, maintenance, usage and end of life phase. Each phase offers opportunities for minimising carbon footprint and therefore represents a distinct planetary impact area, which can be enacted by choosing re-used, recycled or low-carbon materials, balancing between on-site and off-site processing, reducing waste, avoiding demolition by retrofitting, building renewable energy capacity, increasing overall durability – and much more.

Life Cycle Assessment (LCA) is a well-established tool that can reveal the sources of major contributions of carbon footprints and therefore guide the most important reduction interventions. In addition to carbon, urban development activity also emits and uses other undesirable entities such as pollutants, particulates, nutrients, plastics and more which need to be as seriously treated as carbon footprint.

Healthy Ecosystems

Ecosystems stabilise the global climate. However, unlike for climate, there is not a single variable that could measure and fully represent the quality of well-functioning ecosystems, nor a simple way to link the global and local scales. Ecosystems are inherently different to climate. They depend on the combination of highly bio-diverse life, appropriate climate conditions and unspoiled local habitat. Within that biodiversity clean water and soils, balanced biogeochemical flows, access to freshwater, and minimal levels of pollution not least from novel entities. The local and the global ecosystems are connected through species' activities and flow of matter carried by wind patterns and ocean currents.

Therefore, urban development activities lead to local consequences for ecosystems first and then these impact spreads to the global network of ecosystems. As for climate, impacts on ecosystems must be addressed both in the on-site development (local aspirations lens) and at the planetary level (global responsibility lens), throughout the entire supply chain, up and downstream, with ambitious regenerative practices.

These practices need to go beyond narrow green solutions that solely focus on the climate impact and address interconnected ecosystem perspectives as well. Human development has reached the point at which it cannot afford to degrade or lose more ecosystems without hampering its own development.

Urban development has a choice to move away from destroying, degrading, polluting, and fragmenting natural habitat and biodiversity, and instead choose to design for clean outdoor air, regenerate ecosystems and implement ambitious nature-based solutions.

The ecological ceiling of the Doughnut for Urban Development

The ecological ceiling of the Doughnut for Urban Development details 24 local and 24 global impact areas across the two core Earth systems of climate stability and healthy ecosystems. Alongside the impact areas we have mapped and listed impact methodologies and tool, and built a 'Doughnut for Urban Development Database', which we hope will enable actors to create buildings with a more holistic and informed vision.

In some areas such as "E05 - Energy Efficiency" the list of tools, indicators and benchmarks found in existing work is long and impossible to fully capture. In other areas such as "E33 - Support biodiverse soil", existing work is limited and we have been challenged when developing the framework. This may be due to the novelty of including biodiversity in the scope of building design. The impact areas fall under the categories of climate stability and healthy ecosystems, each subdivided by local and global impact areas.

In the following pages we unroll the Ecological ceiling, to define the impact areas, and we give an example of the type of indicator you can use to measure this impact areas. We use building cases to give an example of how you can apply the design principles detailed in these impact areas. None of these cases hit each and every one of the 48 impact areas, but all provide tangible evidence of how you can begin integrating Doughnut principles in your next project.

LOCAL / GLOBAL
In order to apply Doughnut principles we must oscillate between designing for ecological impact locally and ecological impact globally

IMPACT AREAS
The 48 impact areas organised by 12 climate stability local and 12 climate stability global, and 12 healthy ecosystems local and 12 healthy ecosystems global.

CATEGORIES
The ecological ceiling is organised by two categories: on top, climate stability and on the bottom, healthy ecosystems.

PLANETARY BOUNDARIES
The original 9 planetary boundaries are included in the ecological ceiling but do not relate directly to specific impact areas.

ECOLOGICAL CEILING
The 2 categories and 48 ecological impact areas make up the ecological ceiling of the Doughnut for Urban Development.

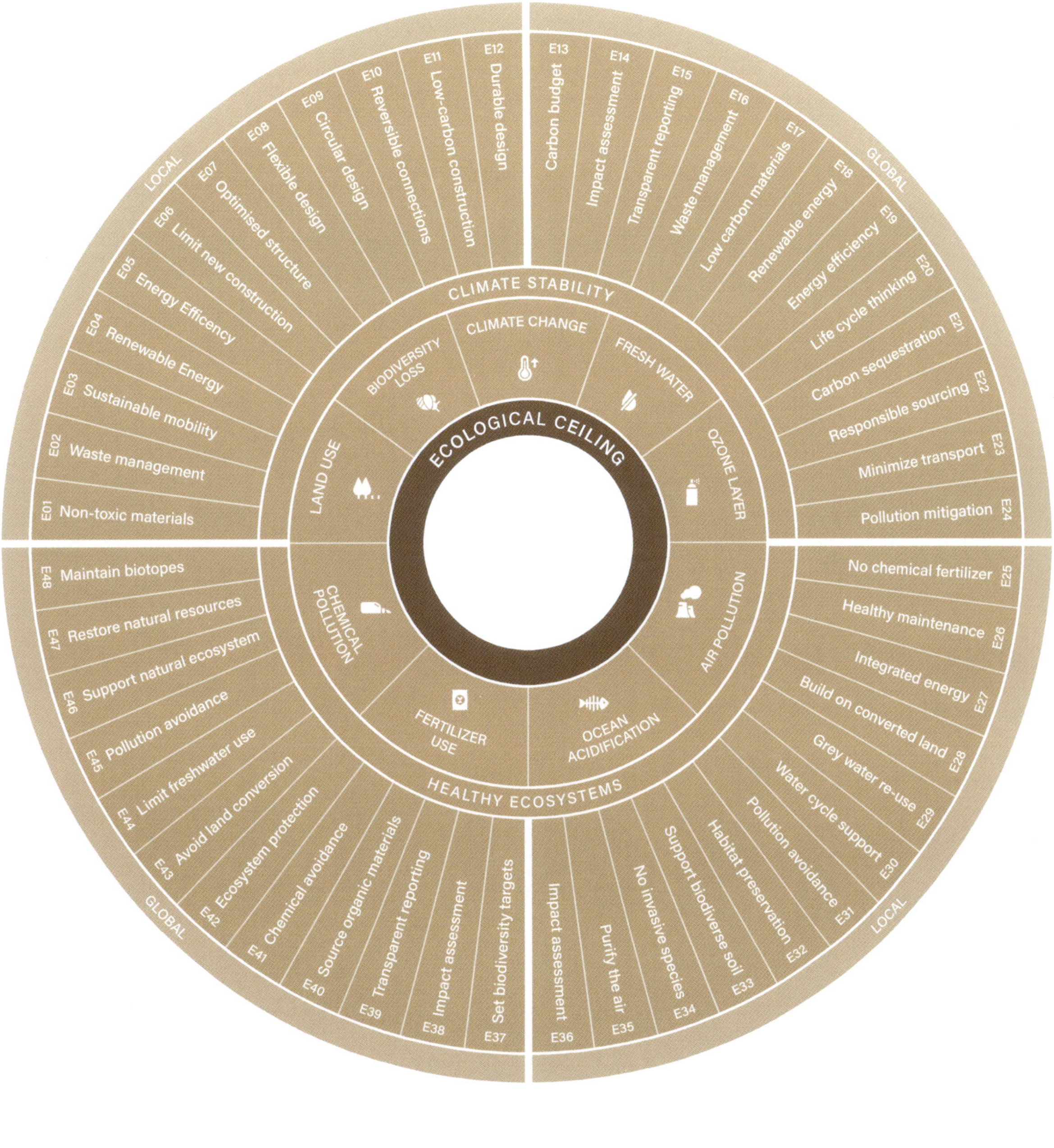

Figure 20: Local and global impact areas in the ecological ceiling of the Doughnut for Urban Development

ECOLOGICAL CEILING
CLIMATE STABILITY / LOCAL

Climate Stability Local

In the realm of urban development, achieving climate stability at the local level involves implementing various strategies on-site. This entails making well-informed procurement decisions, employing effective management practices, and incorporating thoughtful design choices that prioritise climate stability. Additionally, developing sustainable infrastructure and optimising operational energy design are essential components in ensuring climate stability throughout the project's lifetime. By integrating these measures into urban development projects can make significant contributions to mitigating climate impacts and fostering a resilient and sustainable future.

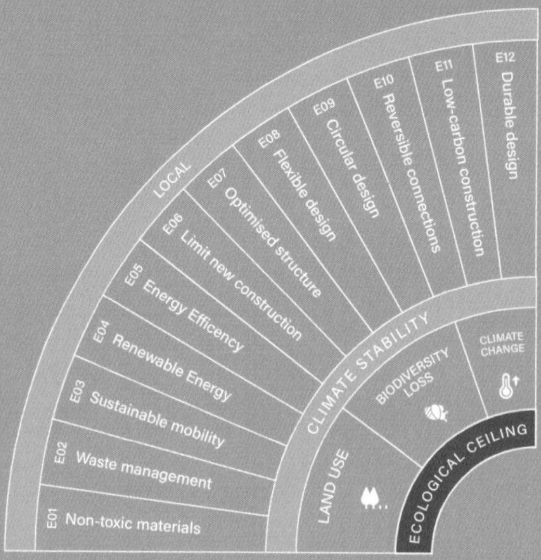

Case Study: The Swan
Impact Areas: E01, E02, E09

The Swan exemplifies responsible urban development with a strong focus on local climate stability. It embraces climate stability through the use of sustainable materials, circular design principles, waste management, and non-toxic materials. The project demonstrates a forward-thinking approach and aligns with indicators such as "E02 - Waste management" and "E09 - Circular design" by up-cycling old materials and giving them new value. Its reliance on recycled materials also enables the principles of "E01 - Non-toxic materials" and "E06 - Limit new construction" By adopting these strategies, The Swan effectively reduces waste, carbon emissions, and positively contributes to the local ecosystem.

City: Gladsaxe . Developer: Gladsaxe Municipality. Architect: Lendager
Year: 2022. Size: 1.436 m2

LOCAL

E01: Non-toxic materials
Use non-toxic, non-harmful building materials to ensure the long-term health and safety of labourers, tenants and natural environment. Specify low-voc and low off-gassing materials and when possible specify certified materials, such as 'Cradle to Cradle' and the 'Nordic Swan' label.

Example Indicator
% of low-VOC & certified materials

E02: Waste management
Specify products that are manufactured efficiently using additive design principles. Minimise on-site construction waste by designing with standard dimensions. Design a circular construction site to ensure material reuse.

Example Indicator
Amount of waste leaving site during construction

E03: Sustainable mobility
Develop on building sites that are well connected to public transportation to promote sustainable mobility practices such as walking, cycling, use of public transportation and ride-share options.

Example Indicator
Proximity to public transportation and alternative modes

E04: Renewable energy
Connect to renewable energy infrastructure for the construction site and the buildings operational phase to reduce dependency on fossil fuels. Where it makes sense from an LCA perspective, integrate energy production on-site.

Example Indicator
% of renewable energy and on-site production

E05: Energy efficiency
Reduce energy consumption in operation through design for passive heating and cooling, specify energy efficient, motion censored systems, and energy saving appliances. Design an active building envelope for heat retention and energy exchange. Use smart systems to identify areas of inefficiency with real-time data.

Example Indicator
Real-time energy measurement during operations

E06: Limit new construction
Limit new construction. Reduce dependency on virgin materials and minimise carbon emissions by utilising the existing building stock as a material bank. Maintain, preserve and re-use culturally significant and environmentally valuable buildings, elements and materials.

Example Indicator
Quantity of reused and preserved materials from existing buildings

E07: Optimised structure
Optimise structural dimensions and design to reduce material usage. Avoid over dimensioning and structural redundancy. Design the structure to have a long life, and loose fit.

Example Indicator
Reduction in materials achieved through optimized design

E08: Flexible design
Optimise building design for flexible use of space to reduce the need for new construction and allow for functional changes in use over time – in both short periods (daily, weekly) through shared spaces and double programming and longer periods where the buildings typology can change.

Example Indicator
Rate of building design flexibility for adaptable space

E09: Circular design
Design circular buildings to promote the preservation of material structural, thermal, environmental, and aesthetic value. Design with a digital twin and material passports to maintain material knowledge and accurately document lifespans.

Example Indicator
Ratio of projects with digital twins & material passports

E10: Reversible connections
Preserve material resources by designing for disassembly using reversible connections, circular building elements, and when possible, product service systems. When specifying technical (non-biogenic) elements use durable, high quality materials to ensure long lifespans.

Example Indicator
% of building elements designed for disassembly and durability

E11: Low-carbon construction
Promote circular and low-carbon construction sites by designing high quality waste handling practices and low-carbon machinery and construction techniques.

Example Indicator
Quantity of circular and low-carbon practices implemented on construction sites

E12: Durable design
Design for durability, easy maintenance, and accessible repair to reduce the need for material exchange. Use appropriate and specific levels of material durability for the given function. For example, a high trafficked entrance will need a more durable material than a living space.

Example Indicator
Documentation rate of building projects with material durability and repair instructions

ECOLOGICAL CEILING
CLIMATE STABILITY / GLOBAL

Climate Stability Global

When it comes to global implications, climate stability in urban development reaches beyond the local scale. It requires taking into account global carbon budgets and targets, adhering to international agreements, embracing a life cycle thinking approach, and implementing strategies that extend beyond the immediate site. This entails considering off-site factors such as the production, procurement, and transportation of materials, as well as energy generation and waste management. By addressing these broader considerations, urban development can contribute to global efforts in achieving climate stability and support the transition to a more sustainable future.

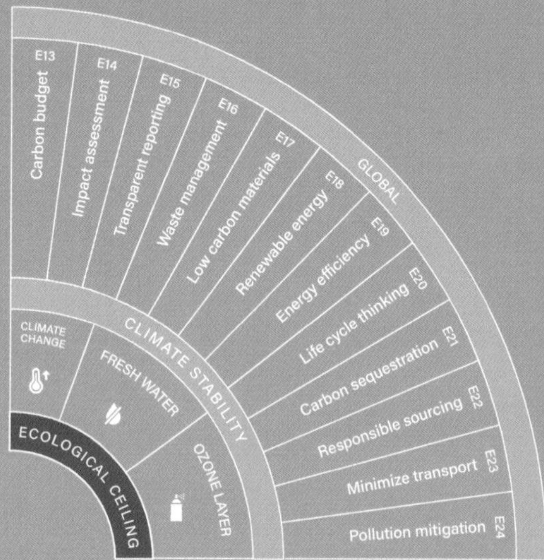

Case Study: VELUX Living Places
Impact Categories: E13, E14, E15

VELUX Living Places is a pioneering initiative that places a strong emphasis on promoting healthy and sustainable living environments. With a global perspective on climate stability, this project strives to minimise its environmental impact by aligning with the Reduction Roadmap (2022) and specifically the "E13 - Carbon budget". To ensure a thorough analysis of its environmental footprint, the initiative incorporates industry standards like Building LCA and the "E14 - Impact assessment." Additionally, transparency is of great significance to VELUX Living Places as it actively promotes transparent reporting as per the "E15 - Transparent reporting" indicator to drive positive change within the industry. VELUX Living Places matches market price for single family home and row-houses and has a strong focus on indoor air quality and daylighting.

City: Copenhagen, Developer: VELUX Group, Architect: EFFEKT, Engineer: Artelia, Contractor: Enemaerke & Petersen, Year: 2023

GLOBAL

E13: Carbon budget
Set and comply with a carbon budget to ensure that your building project is within the planetary boundary for climate change. Use measurable targets to scale your building project within planetary limits.

Example Indicator
Compliance rate with carbon budget targets by assessing carbon footprint

E14: Impact assessment
Comply with relevant industry standards (such as Building LCA) for impact assessment. Relevancy is dependent on local / national frameworks for benchmarking building projects. Benchmarking building projects allows for project comparison and tracking of innovation progress.

Example Indicator
Achievement rate from recognized impact assessment standards and frameworks

E15: Transparent reporting
Be transparent in the documentation and reporting of the building impact assessment. Open source your novel innovations and best practice cases. Stay accountable and follow through on goals to scale building activity within planetary boundaries.

Example Indicator
Transparency rate in impact assessments

E16: Waste management
Promote resource reuse and efficient production to minimise supply chain waste in material extraction, production, and transportation to reduce negative environmental impacts.

Example Indicator
Quantity of reused resources and waste generated in the supply chain

E17: Low carbon materials
Source regional, low-carbon, biogenic, rapidly renewable, and regenerative building materials. Use reputable suppliers who comply with Environmental Product Declarations (EPD) standards.

Example Indicator
Ratio of low-carbon and renewable materials sourced from EPD-compliant suppliers

E18: Renewable energy
Specific building materials from suppliers who use renewable energy in extraction, manufacturing, and production processes across the supply chain to actively limit dependency on fossil fuel.

Example Indicator
% of building materials utilizing renewable energy in the supply chain

E19: Energy efficiency
Minimise energy consumption in extraction, manufacturing, and production processes. Identify energy- intensive processes across the supply chain and optimise those with energy-efficient equipment, efficient design process, waste reduction, automated systems, and smart controls.

Example Indicator
Rate of energy consumption reduction in extraction, manufacturing, and production

E20: Life cycle thinking
Adopt a life cycle perspective from the beginning of the design process by using LCA and LCCs to enable smart, qualified decision making to gain new knowledge about building design and ultimately lower building impact.

Example Indicator
Number of life cycle assessments and life cycle cost analysis conducted in design

E21: Carbon sequestering
Source materials with high-carbon sequestering qualities to use the building as a carbon sink, while minimising the buildings' carbon footprint.

Example Indicator
Quantity of carbon sequestered by building materials used in construction

E22: Responsible sourcing
Source certified and reputable materials that ensure long-term planetary health by minimising environmental impact such as deforestation, water pollution and resource exploitation.

Example Indicator
% of materials sourced from certified and reputable suppliers

E23: Minimise transportation
Minimise transportation impact through extraction, manufacturing, and production processes in the supply chain by specifying regional materials and working with suppliers whose operations are locally based. Specify light-weight materials, elements, and structural systems - transported with electric vehicles.

Example Indicator
Ratio of regional materials used and transportation-related emissions

E24: Pollution mitigation
Mitigate pollution by avoiding the use of materials with dangerous chemical content, thereby ensuring the long-term health of workers and natural environments across the supply chain.

Example Indicator
Quantity of materials used with minimized dangerous chemical content

ECOLOGICAL CEILING
HEALTHY ECOSYSTEMS / LOCAL

Healthy Ecosystems Local

In the pursuit of promoting healthy ecosystems through local urban development, various strategies can be implemented to enhance and restore biodiversity and nature on-site. This involves making deliberate design decisions that minimise the use of chemical fertilisers, prioritize sustainable maintenance practices, re-purpose converted land for construction, safeguard existing habitats, and prevent pollution. By integrating these approaches into urban development projects, cities play a pivotal role in nurturing thriving ecosystems that support a wide array of plant and animal species. These strategies contribute to ecological equilibrium, enrich the natural environment, and yield numerous benefits, including improved air and water quality, heightened resilience to climate change, and enhanced overall well-being for both human inhabitants and wildlife populations.

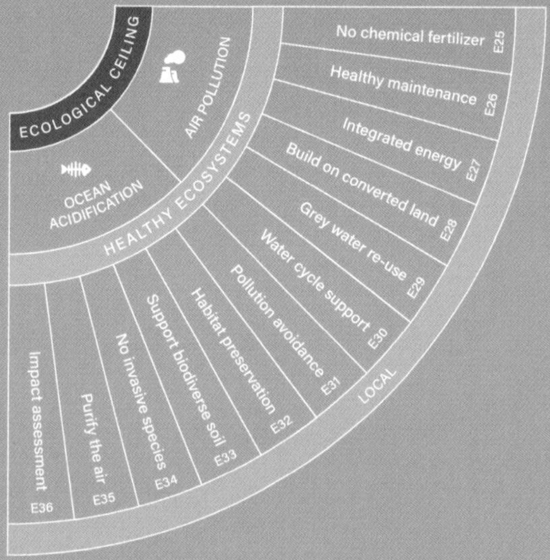

Case Study: CPH Village Jernbanebyen
Impact Categories: E28, E36

CPH Village's new student housing in Jernbanebyen embodies a commitment to local healthy ecosystems, boasting wooden structure housing nestled amidst greenery and thriving wildlife vegetation. It is built in an area previously used for infrastructure logistics. The project site was covered by spontaneous vegetation and some large trees, partly planted, partly self-grown aligning with "E28 - Build on converted land." A biodiversity baseline survey was conducted, which guided the landscape design so that large trees were preserved where possible, living or lying for decomposition, and new vegetation established with native local species aligning with "E36 - Impact assessment."

City: Copenhagen. Developer: CPH Village. Architect: SLA, Arcgency. Year: 2020. Size: 4100 m2

LOCAL

E25: No chemical fertilisers
Avoid the use of chemical fertilisers in the maintenance of open spaces and landscapes to stop eutrophication associated with runoff, thereby protecting the health of lakes, rivers, and other natural water resources.

Example Indicator
% of chemical fertiliser-free landscape maintenance practices

E26: Healthy maintenance
Avoid contaminants such as chemicals, plastics, NOx and SOx that harm on-site biodiversity and biosphere and fair.

Example Indicator
% of maintenance practices without contaminants harmful to on-site biodiversity

E27: Integrated energy
Avoid the use of land for local energy production and incorporate building-integrate renewable energy solutions such as solar PVCs on the buildings roof.

Example Indicator
% on-site energy from building-integrated renewableS, minimizing

E28: Build on converted land
Build high density developments, on already converted land. Do not develop greenfields, forests, or agricultural land suitable for natural restoration.

Example Indicator
Ratio of buildings on converted land vs. greenfields/agricultural land

E29: Grey water use
Conserve natural water resources by designing for the treatment and reuse of greywater on-site for purposes such as irrigation, toilet flushing, cooling systems, and watering non-edible plants.

Example Indicator
Quantity of greywater treated and reused on-site for various purposes

E30: Water cycle support
Support natural water cycles on-site by catching and cleaning water with permeable surfaces, natural cleansing systems such as reed beds, bioswales and "living machines" and redistributing clean water to the local water reserves.

Example Indicator
Quantity of water captured, cleaned, and redistributed on-site through natural systems

E31: Pollution avoidance
Avoid the pollution and disturbance of the local, natural ecosystem by avoiding artificial light pollution, noise pollution, and chemical pollution surrounding the building site.

Example Indicator
Compliance with pollution avoidance measures (light, noise, chemicals)

E32: Habitat preservation
Preserve and support the existing natural habitats and species diversity while designing new habitats that support local biodiversity. Use nature-based solutions in infrastructure such as parking, pathways, roofs, walls, water ways, gardens and the like.

Example Indicator
% of nature-based solutions integrated into infrastructure design

E33: Support biodiverse soil
Preserve natural, biodiverse soil on-site using phytoremediation and composting. By preserving soil, you contribute to maintaining a healthy ecosystems.

Example Indicator
Ratio of preserved biodiverse soil through phytoremediation and composting

E34: No invasive species
Maintain natural green spaces and monitor for invasive species. Work to remove non-locally adapted and invasive species when necessary.

Example Indicator
Compliance with invasive species monitoring and removal protocols

E35: Purify the air
Use photocatalytic coatings such as trees and other nature-based solutions to purify outdoor air quality, while improving thermal comfort and mitigating noise pollution.

Example Indicator
Rate of outdoor air purification using coatings and nature-based solutions

E36: Impact assessment
Engage with qualified, local, expert ecologist to conduct standardised and reputable biodiversity impact assessments on-site.

Example Indicator
Number of on-site biodiversity assessments conducted by qualified ecologists

ECOLOGICAL CEILING
HEALTHY ECOSYSTEMS / GLOBAL

Healthy Ecosystems Global

Promoting healthy ecosystems through urban development has a global impact that extends beyond local boundaries, considering off-site factors and adopting a life cycle thinking approach. It involves implementing strategies to enhance biodiversity and nature on a global scale by embracing sustainable practices, preserving natural resources, mitigating pollution, and setting biodiversity targets. By incorporating nature-based solutions like sustainable land use planning, urban development can contribute to the preservation and restoration of ecosystems worldwide. Urban development can play a crucial role in safeguarding biodiversity and fostering a sustainable planet. These actions have profound benefits, including climate regulation, water resource management, and the preservation of vital ecosystem services that support life on Earth.

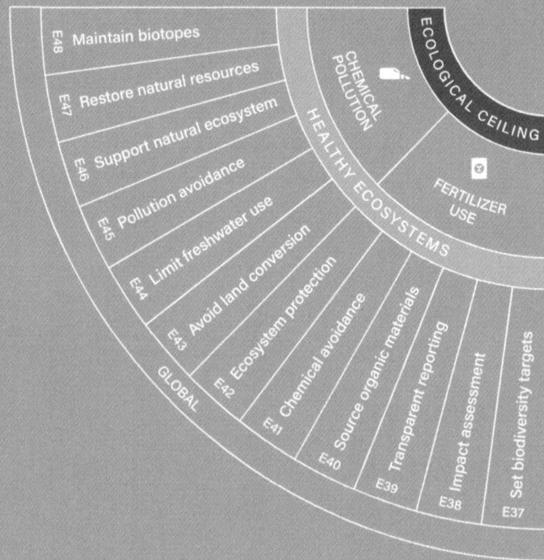

Case Study: Kajstaden Tall Timber Building
Impact Categories: E40, E41

The Kajstaden Tall Timber Building prioritises the integration of healthy ecosystems in urban development with a global perspective. It showcases this commitment, by sourcing local organic materials, particularly timber, and promoting sustainable construction practices, aligning with the "E40 - Source organic materials" indicator. The project exemplifies the potential of tall timber buildings constructed mainly with wood as a sustainable alternative to conventional construction methods. It emphasises the use of locally available materials, in line with the principles of chemical avoidance during transportation as outlined in "E41 - Chemical avoidance".

City: Västerås. Developer: Trenum Västerås AB. Architect: C.F. Møller. Year: 2019. Size: 2.400 m2

GLOBAL

E37: Set biodiversity target
Set and comply with a biodiversity target to ensure your building project impact is within planetary limits for biodiversity and works towards the regeneration of a healthy ecosystems.

Example Indicator
Compliance with biodiversity targets for ecosystem regeneration

E38: Impact Assessment
Engage with qualified, local, expert ecologists to conduct standardised and reputable biodiversity impact assessments off-site.

Example Indicator
Number of off-site biodiversity assessments conducted by qualified ecologists

E39: Transparent reporting
Be transparent in the documentation and reporting of the building impact assessment. Share your novel innovations and good cases.

Example Indicator
Transparency in impact assessments and documentation of innovative practices

E40: Source organic materials
Source organic materials that are grown without the use of chemical fertilisers in the supply chain, to minimse impact on local ecosystems.

Example Indicator
% of organic materials sourced from chemical-free supply chains

E41: Chemical avoidance
Avoid pollution by limiting the use of chemicals and plastics in the production and transportation of building materials.

Example Indicator
Reduction in chemical and plastic usage in building material production

E42: Ecosystem protection
Reduce extraction of virgin materials such as rock, sand and timber for the construction of buildings and landscapes to protect natural and healthy ecosystems.

Example Indicator
Reduction in extraction of virgin materials for ecosystem protection

E43: Avoid land conversion
Avoid land conversion for energy production across the supply chain. Procure energy from production sites on already converted land, from suppliers who actively work to regenerate the land.

Example Indicator
Ratio of energy sourced from converted land and regenerative suppliers

E44: Limit freshwater use
Limit the use of groundwater and fresh surface water in the supply chain by using grey water to produce building materials.

Example Indicator
% reduction in freshwater consumption through greywater use

E45: Pollution avoidance
Reduce off-site artificial light, noise pollution, disturbance and chemical pollution of surrounding natural ecosystems across the supply chain.

Example Indicator
Compliance with measures to minimize off-site pollution

E46: Support natural ecosystems
Source building materials that do not reduce habitat quality, genetic diversity, or functional biodiversity.

Example Indicator
% of building materials sourced without compromising biodiversity and habitat quality

E47: Restore natural resources
Restore natural resources and avoid overexploitation by balancing the rate of natural material consumption with the ability of that material to regenerate at a natural rate.

Example Indicator
Ratio of restored resources to consumption considering regeneration capacity

E48: Maintain biotopes
Maintaining biotopes is essential for the preservation of biodiversity, ecological balance, and the sustainable provision of virgin resources, safeguarding unique species and ecological processes that they support, while promoting sustainable land and resource management.

Example Indicator
Compliance with biotope maintenance practices for biodiversity preservation and land management

Urban Development within Planetary Boundaries

04

In this chapter we focus on methods for urban developments to set ecological targets that respect climate stability and healthy ecosystems, and to measure their ecological performance - on-site and off-site - using life cycle assessment (LCA) and other approaches.

We discuss how the allocation of allowable resource or emission shares to individual projects should not be seen as a purely technical exercise - it carries far-reaching and complex ethical implications, which depend critically on the sharing principles applied along each step of the target-setting process.

Given the complex ethical implications, we describe several sharing principle examples commonly used to set ecological targets based on planetary boundaries. With this, we give our view on the extent to which they align with Doughnut principles. We illustrate a target-setting procedure for the Danish urban development context and describe approaches to integrate ecological targets with project-level impact

The Appendix provides more in-depth description of methods used throughout this section, including:

- Literature and explanation on principles to allocate ecological sustainability targets.
- Advanced methods to use LCA to assess such targets.
- Differences between LCA tools and frameworks used in various countries, and some examples of correction factors to account for missing processes in LCA.
- A description of the tools used to assess impact on ecosystems and biodiversity.
- Guidelines on whether and how to use and report carbon offsets, bio-credits and similar schemes to regenerative ends.

According to Doughnut Economics, allocation needs to be regenerative and distributive by design, Therefore allocation principles based on the current economic paradigm are not aligned with Doughnut Economics.

Setting and assessing targets for Climate Change

Figure 21: Setting and assessing targets for climate change

This figure can be used to understand how to set and assess targets for climate change from a global level down to urban development projects and is also indicative of how this section of the book is laid out.

The following section of the book explores several approaches to allocation. In the context of this book, allocation refers to the process of assigning or distributing a share of specific planetary boundaries to national, sectoral, and project level scales. The aim is to ensure urban development in a given place, stays within its respective share of the climate change planetary boundary.

Allocation is not just a mathematical science but rather a subjective and inherently political pursuit. Allocation is useful in setting targets but should not be done in a vacuum. It is important to be context aware and consider the other tools and indicators that are used in the building industry for target setting and benchmarking impact. For example, the allocation approaches presented in the forthcoming sections do not align with standard Building LCA, because the account for different processes. As such, the targets presented cannot be compared directly to Building LCA without applying a correction factor.

We can and should use climate science to set measurable targets in the building industry. It is quite clear that we need to reduce our impacts and setting measurable targets will help urban developers make qualified design decisions on the path towards a regenerative future. It is important to remember systems level thinking when we set reduction targets. Project level, bottom-up target should be complemented by national-level, top-down limits to industry growth if urban development should move towards the safe and just space for humanity.

First, the finite planetary boundary for climate change is identified.

That boundary is translated into a safe operating space, or target for annual global emissions.

A share of the annual global emissions is allocated to a country. In this case, Denmark.

A share of the annual Danish emissions target is allocated to the building sector and then down to project level targets.

Building LCA can be used to assess the climate change impact of a building.

LCA results should be adjusted for missing processes.

Regenerative measures should be implemented both on and off-site.

Planetary sustainability will be reached when we learn to use urban development to restore planetary health.

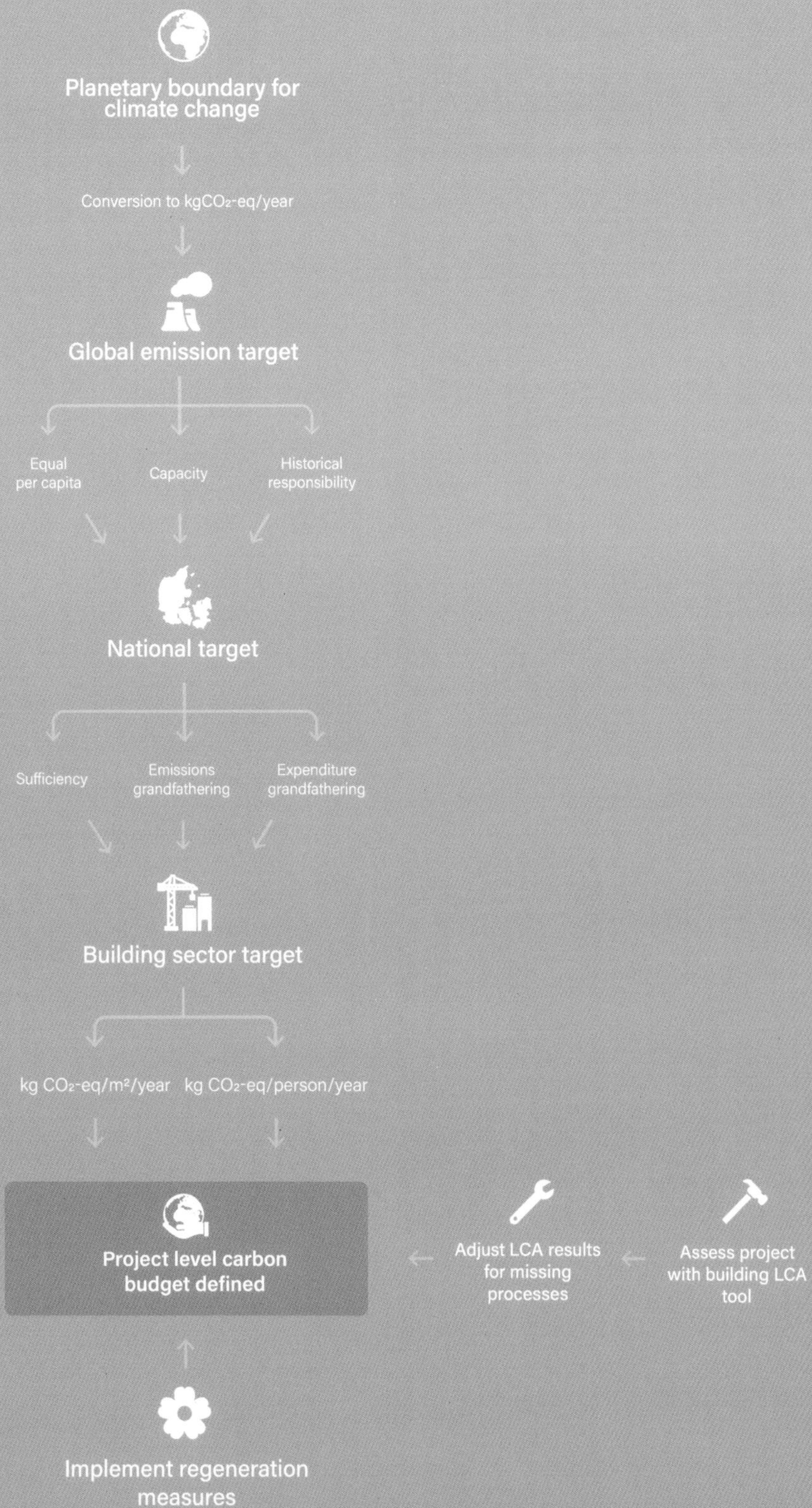

Planetary boundary for climate change
Conversion to kgCO₂-eq/year
Global emission target
Equal per capita
Capacity
Historical responsibility
National target
Sufficiency
Emissions grandfathering
Expenditure grandfathering
Building sector target
kg CO₂-eq/m²/year
kg CO₂-eq/person/year
Project level carbon budget defined
Adjust LCA results for missing processes
Assess project with building LCA tool
Implement regeneration measures

Allocating shares of the global climate change boundary to sectors

Climate change is both a planetary boundary and an environmental impact category that can be measured through LCA, but it is expressed in different units across the two frameworks. The planetary boundary for climate change corresponds to an atmospheric concentration of 350 parts per million (ppm) carbon, or a maximum 'radiative forcing' of 1 Watt per square metre (W/m^2) at the top of the atmosphere. Meanwhile, LCA results for climate change are commonly expressed in total greenhouse gases emitted per year, by weight, such as kilograms or tonnes (kg CO_2eq/m^2/year).

The safe operating space for climate change has been converted into common LCA units by using a climate model to calculate the maximum amount of greenhouse gas emissions that could be emitted each year while respecting the 1 W/m^2 boundary in radiative forcing (Bjørn & Hauschild, 2015; Petersen et al., 2022).

This method defines the global safe operating space for climate change as **2.51 billion tonnes of carbon equivalents per year (Gt CO_2-eq/year).** Today we emit approximately 47.9 billion tonnes carbon per year, which means we must reduce global emissions by 96% to get within this safe operating space for climate change.

According to budgets defined in the IPCC AR6 (2021) report, we must do so within the next 5-10 years to stay within the Paris Agreement 1.5°C scenario for global warming with an 83% likelihood of succeeding. If we continue emitting as we do today, we will use up the remaining carbon budget in the next 5 years. If we begin reducing right now, we can extend the reduction time-line until between 2029 – 2036 (Reduction Roadmap, 2022).

Sharing principles for allocating the global climate boundary to nations

In this section, we present three ethically distinct sharing principles used to allocate global boundaries to the national scale: Equal per capita, Capacity, and Historical responsibility (Bjørn et al., 2020; Ryberg et al., 2020; Lucas et al., 2020; Häyhä et al., 2016). Each of these have distinctive ways to address fairness and equity.

We do not include other known principles for allocating national shares, such as Territorial or Acquired rights (also known as 'grandfathering') because such allocation principles – based on the current, highly inequitable, cross-country economic distribution – are not aligned with the core regenerative and distributive principles of Doughnut Economics.

The general allocation approach applied in this study could be adapted to another planetary boundary and to other countries using pertinent data. To better understand the details, data and calculations presented in this chapter, visit the Appendix Chapter 3.

Equal per capita

The equal per capita principle allocates an equal share of the climate change boundary to all people in the world on an annual basis. The rationale is that all human beings should be entitled to access an equal share of the atmospheric commons.

However, allocating equal shares per capita will not give equal opportunities, given wide cross-country disparities in terms of national capacities to meet the needs of their residents and historical responsibilities for destabilising the climate. For these reasons, an equal allocation per capita is not well-aligned with Doughnut Economics, but it is included here for reference because it is one of the most widely used allocation principles in the literature.

When we apply the equal per capita sharing principle we find that Denmark is allocated 0.076% of the annual global climate change boundary, because Denmark is 0.076% of the global population (as of 2019).

Capacity

The capacity principle expands upon the equal per capita principle by also taking into account income levels. It allocates a smaller share of the climate boundary on an annual basis to the wealthiest countries (measured in GDP per capita). The rationale behind this principle is that the wealthiest countries already have the socio-technical capacity required to meet their residents' needs, while also making the changes necessary to carry out emission reductions.

The capacity principle is more in line with the principles of Doughnut Economics than the equal per capita principle since it favours countries with the highest social shortfalls. However, it does not consider a nation's historical responsibility for causing climate change.

When we apply the capacity principle we find that Denmark is allocated 0.009% of the annual global climate change boundary. Because Denmark's GDP per capita is relatively high, Denmark is given a smaller share than with equal per capita.

Historical responsibility

The historical responsibility principle recognises that the rising concentration of carbon in the atmosphere is a cumulative problem, and allocates the largest share of the climate change boundary to the countries who have historically contributed the least to climate change (e.g. from 1990 to 2018). Likewise, the countries that have historically contributed the most to climate change are entitled to the smallest share of future emissions.

When we apply the historical responsibility principle we find that Denmark is allocated -0.07% of the annual global climate boundary, due to Denmark's historically high level of carbon emissions per capita.

The negative share means that Denmark is in "climate debt." This raises the difficult question of whether (and how much) high-emitting countries like Denmark should compensate countries that have remained within their fair share for their "atmospheric appropriation" (Fanning & Hickel, 2023).

Historical responsibility is the principle most aligned with Doughnut Economics because it holds accountable historically high-emitting nations and makes evident their responsibility to carry out more ambitious regenerative practices in the future.

Sharing principles for allocating national climate budgets to sectors

Now that the global boundary has been allocated to the national scale, it can be further divided at a sectoral level. In this section, we introduce three sharing principles that can be applied: Expenditure grandfathering, Emissions grandfathering, and Sufficiency. They can be used to allocate national shares of the climate change boundary to sectoral activities, such as housing.

In the context of this book we focus on the human right to housing. The three sharing principles presented here account for "housing" through three unique lenses. The results are therefore not directly comparable to each other, because they measure different things.

Expenditure grandfathering

The expenditure grandfathering principle is widely used to allocate sectoral shares of the climate boundary in the literature. It is based on the rationale that current household and government expenditures can be used to illustrate how much people value different consumption categories.

However, it is well-established that current consumption patterns are not sustainable, especially

	Housing (kg CO_2-eq/year)	Expenditures grandfathering	Emissions grandfathering	Sufficiency
Per m^2	**Equal per capita**	0.90	1.01	**1.18**
	Capacity	0.11	0.13	0.15
	Historical responsibility	-0.80	-0.90	**-1.06**

	Housing (kg CO_2-eq/year)	Expenditures grandfathering	Emissions grandfathering	Sufficiency
Per person	**Equal per capita**	45.67	51.31	**60.43**
	Capacity	5.85	6.57	7.73
	Historical responsibility	-40.77	-45.81	**-53.95**

Figure 22: This table presents nine project level carbon budgets proposed in this section. The top table presents targets measured in kg CO_2eq/m^2/year with the lowest share being -1.06 and the highest share being 1.18 kg CO_2eq/m_2/year. The bottom table presents project level carbon budgets presented in this chapter measured in kg CO_2eq/per person/year with the lowest share being -53.95 and the highest share being 60.43kg CO_2eq/person/year.

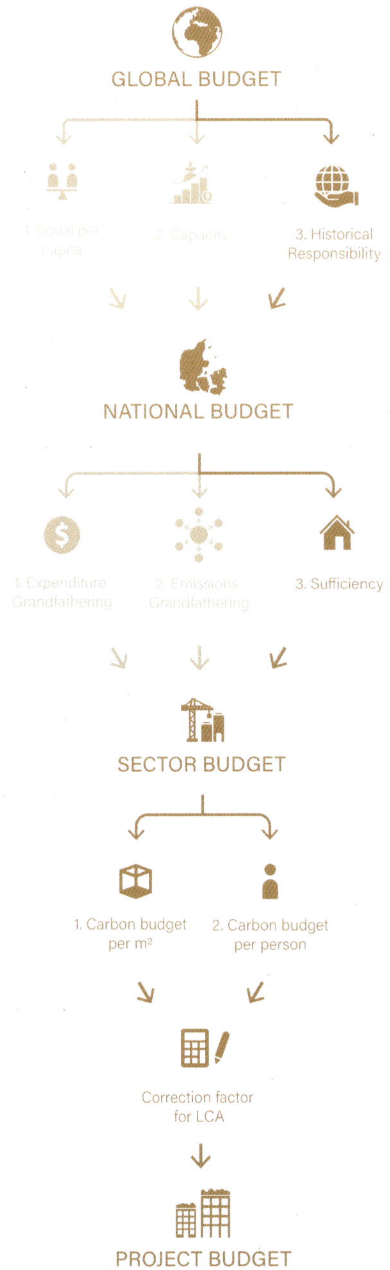

Figure 23: This illustration defines one of the nine potential project level budgets presented in this chapter. As an example, we've selected the sharing principles that were described as "most aligned with Doughnut Economics," which consequentially represents the lowest share of -1.06 kg CO_2eq/m^2/year and -53.95 kg CO_2eq/person/year.

in high-income countries, so we see little reason to expect that allocating sectoral shares based on current consumption category expenditures would lead to a more sustainable consumption pattern.

Rather, we believe that regenerative and distributive principles aligned with the Doughnut will require scaling-down wasteful and divisive activity expenditures, especially those enabling luxury consumption and elite accumulation of wealth, while scaling-up expenditures in other much-needed activities, such as universal basic services provisioning and the green energy transition.

As such, the expenditure grandfathering principle is not well-aligned with the principles of Doughnut Economics, though it is often applied out of convenience due to the widely available national economic data on the final consumption expenditure of households, governments, and gross capital formation.

When we apply the expenditure grandfathering to the Danish context we find that 21.5% of the annual national climate change budget is allocated to housing. Expenditure grandfathering considers how much of our annual income we spend on housing. What housing includes, is less defined. It may include things like furniture, rent or taxes related to housing.

Emissions grandfathering

The Emissions grandfathering principle has a similar rationale, strengths, and shortcomings to expenditure grandfathering, and it is also widely used in the literature due to data availability. This principle generally allocates sectoral shares of a national carbon budget based on each sector's share of total greenhouse gas emissions, cumulatively over a given period or on an annual basis. For instance, if the construction sector currently contributes 20% of national emissions, it would be allocated the same share in the future. However, like expenditure grandfathering, this principle grants preferential treatment to incumbent large-scale sectors, to the detriment of smaller and emerging initiatives that may embody a far more regenerative and distributive design.

The Emissions grandfathering principle is thus not well-aligned with the principles of Doughnut Economics, as it maintains the current composition of emissions across sectors and could give rise to a perverse incentive of rewarding actors that make no efforts to reduce emissions.

When emissions grandfathering is applied in a Danish context 15.4% of the annual national climate change budget is allocated to housing. Emissions grandfathering includes the emissions from activities like building renovations, development, maintenance and even energy used when allocating a share to housing.

Sufficiency

The sufficiency principle acknowledges that people have multiple needs that must be met to be able to participate meaningfully in society with dignity, but those needs are not infinite and, crucially, they can be fulfilled. In this view, it makes little sense to continue dedicating resources beyond a given sufficiency threshold for provisioning food, housing, education, mobility and so on. There is growing momentum around this principle, including in the latest IPCC Synthesis Report (2022), which defines sufficiency as "a set of measures and daily practices that avoid demand for energy, materials, land, and water while delivering human well-being for all within planetary boundaries."

We propose a novel method to allocate sectoral shares based on the sufficiency principle. We build on a study (Millward-Hopkins et al., 2020) that estimates the minimum energy required for living "decent lives" across different consumption categories, such as food, housing, healthcare, and others. We argue that the shares of minimum energy required for decent living across these categories can be used to allocate sufficiency-based sectoral shares to the housing sector of a given country (e.g. Denmark).

Out of the three principles for sectoral allocation presented here, the sufficiency principle is most aligned with the principles of Doughnut Economics because it is based directly on the satisfaction of human needs. This is a completely new approach to allocation and the specific shares may be adjusted in future work, as experience and feedback to using this approach are gained.

When we apply sufficiency to the Danish context we find that 15.1% of the annual national climate change budget is allocated to housing. Sufficiency includes emissions from activities such as housing construction, thermal comfort levels, illumination and water heating among other factors when allocating a share to housing.

From global climate boundary to the Danish urban development sector

To scale from sector level to project level two approaches are taken. The first approach is based on the existing Danish building stock, scaling the project budget down to an indicator of kg CO_2eq /m²/year. The second approach is based on the current Danish population, scaling project budget down to an indicator of kg CO_2/person/year.

The benefit to applying two project level budgets is that we have a holistic approach to safe guard against overconsumption. When we set budgets based on m² limit, we ensure that the embodied and operational energy of the building is within planetary boundaries for climate change. When we set a budget based on a per person limit we mitigate living in excess in the future. The m² limit tends to be more actionable for building industry practitioners who use carbon budgets in the design and specification of materials, whereas the per person limit helps developers and individuals make informed decisions about how much space we should occupy in the future.

The project level shares include a range of nine different project level carbon budgets from -1.06 kg CO_2/ m²/year to 1.18 kg CO_2/ m²/year, and nine different project level carbon budgets from -53.96 kg CO_2/person/year to 60.43 kg CO_2/person/year as shown in **Figure 22**.

These targets should be seen as examples for setting carbon budgets within the planetary boundary for climate change. However, in order to apply these budgets directly to the building project a correction factor will need to be applied.

While the first indicator (kg CO_2eq/m²/year) is the indicator used in Building LCA, it is important to remember that the project level budgets presented in **Figure 22** do not necessarily cover the same scope as common Building LCA tools. Generally speaking, building LCA measures material flows and energy use scenarios to calculate building impact and are quite specific to each project. In contrast, the sectoral sharing principles described in the previous section apply data that measures more abstract measures such as financial flows and sectoral emission trends.

In the following section we present a tenth allocation approach, the Reduction Roadmap, which was created to align with how building impact is measured in Denmark today. As such, the reduction targets set by the Reduction Roadmap can be compared directly to Building LCA results in Denmark.

Allocation in the Danish building industry today

In this section we present the Reduction Roadmap (2022) and the Danish building certification DGNB Planet (2023), which represent two of the first known applications of allocation adopted in the Danish building industry. These examples are evidence of a sectoral shift towards applying absolute sustainability targets within building projects and a shift towards open-sourcing new knowledge for the betterment of the planet.

The Reduction Roadmap

The Reduction Roadmap (Roadmap) is a tenth approach to allocation presented in this book. The Roadmap is a collaborative research project which translates the Paris Agreement and the planetary boundary for climate change into industry-specific reduction targets for new, Danish housing projects. The Roadmap identifies where we are today, where we need to go, and the speed at which we must reduce our carbon emissions to reach Earth's safe operating space (**Figure 26**).

The Roadmap aligns with Danish political frameworks (climate policy and commitment to the Paris Agreement) and technical frameworks (Building LCA) making it an actionable tool for accurately benchmarking reduction progress, within a national context. The Roadmap is an example of a top-down initiative and models reduction targets based on Danish building industry construction trends, or rather based on Emissions grandfathering.

The Roadmap takes the same departure point presented in the former section and defines the global safe operating space for climate change as 2.51 Gt CO_2eq/year (Petersen et al., 2022).

The Roadmap allocation approach aligns consistently with how we measure building impact in Denmark, Building LCA (EN 15978) and is built on the study *Whole Life Carbon Assessment of 60 Buildings: Possibilities to develop benchmark values for LCA of buildings* (Zimmermann et al., 2021), where average emissions of new housing is benchmarked at 9.63kg CO_2-eq/m^2/year.

The Roadmap scales global greenhouse gas emission target levels (2.51 Gt CO_2-eq / year), down to national level using equal per capita sharing principle (Denmark represents 0.075% of global population), to industry level (new housing accounts for 3.3% of Danish national emissions), to new housing (we build approximately 3,072,000 m^2/year) - and finally to a target level (50-year reference period). Assuming we continue with a constant rate of construction in the future, a 96% reduction of 9.63kg CO_2eq/m^2/year corresponds to a target emission level of 0.4 kg CO_2eq/m^2/year (**Figure 25**).

The Roadmap allocation is based upon Emissions grandfathering and therefore does not align with the core principles of Doughnut Economics. The Roadmap does however align with how we measure building impact in Denmark. What this means practically is that the reduction targets set (0.4 kg CO_2eq/m^2/year) does not require a correction factor to compare with Building LCA. It is therefore a suitable approach to benchmark industry progress towards the safe operating space for climate change.

The Roadmap represents a sectoral shift towards adopting absolute targets in the Danish building industry and is changing the way industry actors set project ambitions. An example of this is the DGNB Planet certification.

DGNB Planet

DGNB Planet was first launched by the Danish Green Building Council in 2023 Council. The Danish Green Building Council is a non-profit organisation that promotes sustainable building practices and environmental certification systems in Denmark.

DGNB Planet is a new addition to the many existing certification schemes available through DGNB.

To achieve the DGNB Planet, a project must attain at least the DGNB Silver level and fulfil all 'knock-out criteria.' With the ambition to bring the Danish building industry within the planetary boundaries, DGNB has adopted reduction targets defined by the Reduction Roadmap. Similar to the Reduction Roadmap the DGNB reduction targets will lower over time. From 2023: the target are set to 6.55 kg CO_2eq/m^2/year, from 2025: 5.02 kg CO_2eq/m^2/year, from 2027: 3.45 kg CO_2eq/m^2/year and in 2029: 1.94 kg CO_2eq/m^2/year.

The Reduction Roadmap represents the type of absolute targets needed to scale impact with planetary boundaries. In future iterations DGNB Planet may include other control variables such as limits of carbon per person.

Beyond setting measurable targets DGNB works to create an awareness of what the planetary boundaries are. This includes understanding why respecting them is important, what can be done to stay within them, and how they are an interconnected system. The DGNB Planet seeks to promote awareness and education within the building industry.

A crucial component of raising awareness is sharing best practices demonstrating how far we have come, and to provide knowledge that others can build on. DGNB Planet certification requires building owners to commit to sharing LCA data and their biodiversity strategy. Furthermore the owner should during operations, annually report on energy consumption and document their biodiversity progress. As such, DGNB works to promote knowledge sharing through transparency.

DGNB Planet sees achieving planetary sustainability as a long-term goal. Therefore DGNB Planet must continuously raise its ambitions to push the industry forward. Thus, the knock-out criteria are not static. Rather, they are as ambitious as possible amidst current industry knowledge, with updates expected with updated in the coming DGNB manuals.

The current version of the DGNB Planet has knock-out criteria connected to four out of the nine planetary boundaries: Climate Change, Biodiversity, Land change, and Novel Entities.

The future work of the DGNB Planet will involve building on the Doughnut for Urban Development and work to further define relevant requirements to reducing the negative impact of projects, in relation to the identified planetary boundaries and continuing to share best practice examples with the industry to foster knowledge-sharing and innovation.

In the following section it is explained why Life-Cycle Assessment (LCA) is an essential tool for building industry practitioners to make evidence based decisions and measure building impact in a concise, uniform way.

Figure 24: The DGNB Planet Logo

Level	Today's emissions	Target emissions	Unit
1. Housing m² per year	9.63	0.4	kg CO_2-eq/m²/year
2. Housing m²	482	20	kg CO_2-eq/m²
3. Sector	1.479.168	61.440	tons CO_2-eq/year
4. Share of total Danish emissions	3.3%	3.3%	%

Figure 25: This figure illustrates the allocation factors applied in the Reduction Roadmap.

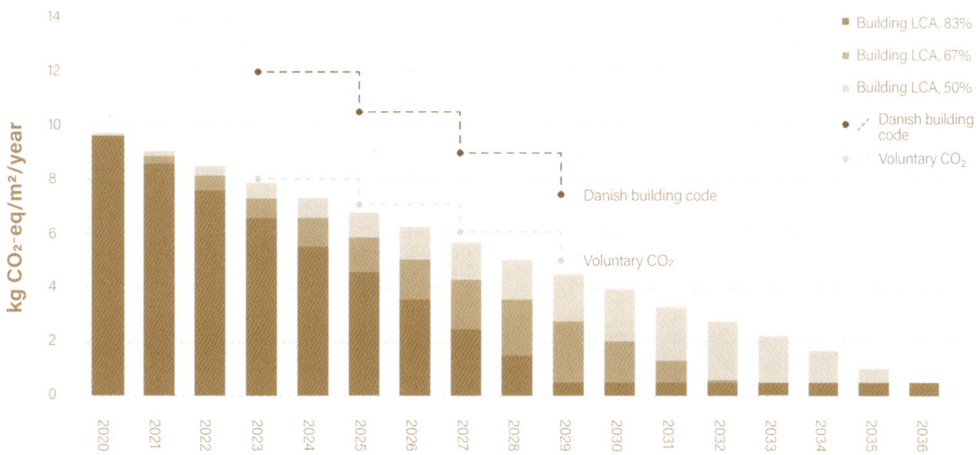

Figure 26: This figure illustrates the reduction pathways for new Danish housing following an 85%, 67% and 50% likelihood for staying with the global warming target of 1.5°C. The safe operating space for housing should be reached between 2029 -2036. The targets set for Danish building regulation (BR18) and the voluntary low emission class are illustrated as a reference point. These are policy measures implemented in 2023 by the Danish government to reduce building emissions.

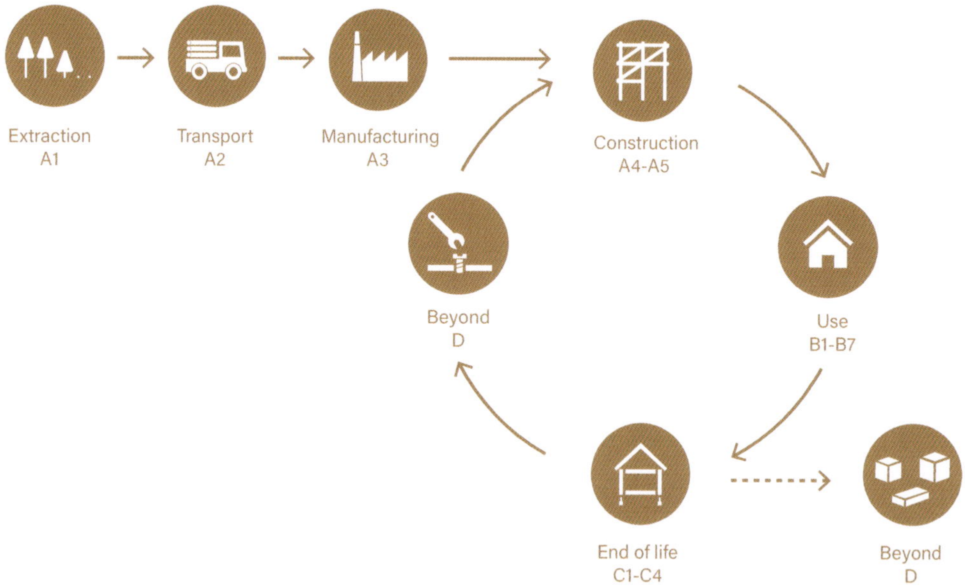

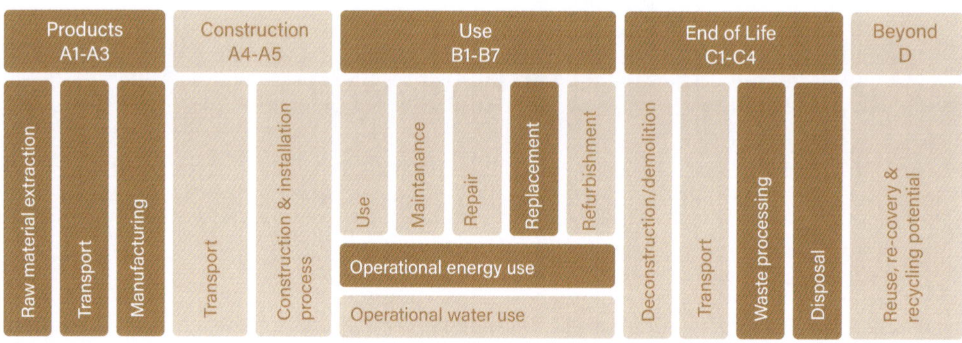

Figure 27: A building's life cycle illustrated two ways. The figure on top represents the circular potential of building materials. The bottom figure is illustrated according to the EN 15804 standard, where areas highlighted in dark brown are currently included in the Danish Building LCA calculation.

Assessing impacts over the entire life cycle

Life-cycle assessment (LCA) is a method to calculate environmental impacts caused by a product or service over its entire life cycle, including the extraction of raw materials, transport, manufacturing, operation, maintenance, and final disposal as illustrated in Figure 27.

In theory, LCA requires listing all processes happening throughout the life cycle, and their corresponding environmental impacts in various categories (global warming, eutrophication, ozone depletion, etc.). In practice, building LCAs are often carried out with dedicated tools, such as OneClickLCA or the Danish tool LCAbyg. These tools include pre-calculated environmental impacts for construction products and processes, and only require the user to enter information on the building's dimensions, energy use and material content. LCA is often used to compare the environmental impacts of entire buildings or specific products. For instance, to assess which façade material is the most environmentally sustainable. It can also be used to assess planetary sustainability targets.

Scope of LCA and of climate stability

When assessing planetary sustainability, we need to ensure that the LCA includes all relevant processes. LCA tools and methods used in various countries for certification or regulation differ in the processes and building parts they cover. Some exclude for instance outdoor works, technical installations, or demolition processes (although there is a trend towards a more and more comprehensive coverage in LCA tools).

Moreover, common LCAs cut off processes very far up the supply chain, such as the manufacturing of mining equipment used to obtain raw materials. As a result, building-level LCAs typically miss some processes that are part of the construction sector.

These truncations are not a major issue when using LCA for certification or regulation. However, they are significant when comparing LCA results to "absolute" targets such as the planetary boundaries, where being comprehensive is important. The Appendix Chapter 2 explains this issue more in-depth and provides an overview of scope differences between countries as well as examples of correction factors to account for missing processes.

Converting LCA results into Planetary Boundary indicators

The allocation processes in this section were based on a conversion of the climate change boundary to an LCA indicator. It is also possible to communicate LCA results in the same indicators as the planetary boundaries. To do so, one must first list all elementary flows to and from the environment happening during the life cycle, and then convert these flows into impacts on each planetary boundary (Ryberg et al., 2018).

This method is described further in the Appendix Chapter 2. The advantage is that it works with most planetary boundaries, but it is more complex and requires detailed LCA tools such as OpenLCA, SimaPro, or 'LCA for Experts' (formerly known as GaBi).

LCA is an important tool for measuring building impact. As detailed above, there are many ways to use LCA to inform the design process. LCA is standardised by location and it's important to align building LCA with standard methods, so that comparison between building projects is easy to do. LCA allows us to work towards carbon reduction targets defined through allocation, but we must remember that common building LCA tools do not always cover the same scope as the allocated project targets. For more on LCA see the Appendix Chapter 2.

The impacts of urban development on healthy ecosystems can be split into local impacts occurring on and around the development site, and remote impacts occurring throughout the global supply chain, linked for instance with the production of construction materials.

Setting and assessing targets for healthy ecosystems

Figure 28: illustrates the assessment process for the planetary boundaries related to healthy ecosystems

Ecosystems and biodiversity are fundamentally different to climate change. While climate change is a global phenomenon where the exact location of the emissions does not affect their consequences, healthy ecosystems are better understood as a multitude of local issues. In other words, the location of the phenomenon matters, and it is not enough to use only a global metric of emissions. Each ecosystem potentially impacted by the development is unique and must be considered. Furthermore, several planetary boundaries are included under the umbrella term of "healthy ecosystems", including biodiversity loss, freshwater availability, land-system change, biogeochemical flows and novel entities. For these reasons, the application of the principles as described previously for climate change do not apply for biodiversity.

Based on the fact that several planetary boundaries related to healthy ecosystems are already transgressed, the overall target is to be "planet positive". This means that developments must implement regenerative measures, give more area to natural ecosystems than they take, improve biodiversity, and restore biogeophysical systems such as freshwater and nutrient cycles. This overall target should be achieved in relevant impact areas at the local scale (where the development takes place), as well as at a global scale (where impacts throughout the supply chain take place).

Just like for climate change, LCA can be used to assess ecosystem impacts over the supply chain, although it requires additional data collection. On the other hand, local impacts are measured and assessed from direct surveys and development plans. The following sections describe how the global control variables for healthy ecosystems can be translated into practical indicators for urban development assessment.

- The planetary boundary for healthy ecosystems is identified. This includes the boundaries for freshwater, pollutants, biodiversity and land-use
- Local biodiversity net gain tool is used to leave the building site more biodiverse after construction than before.
- Off-site biodiversity tool is used to ensure more regeneration than damage over the global supply chain.
- Assess supply chain biodiversity impact with using LCA tools.
- Assess local biodiversity impact based on land use
- Use reputable and verified third-party data on biodiversity impact
- Convert LCA results into biodiversity impacts for the urban development project.
- Regenerative measures should be implemented both on and off-site.
- Planetary sustainability will be reached when we learn to use urban development to restore planetary health.

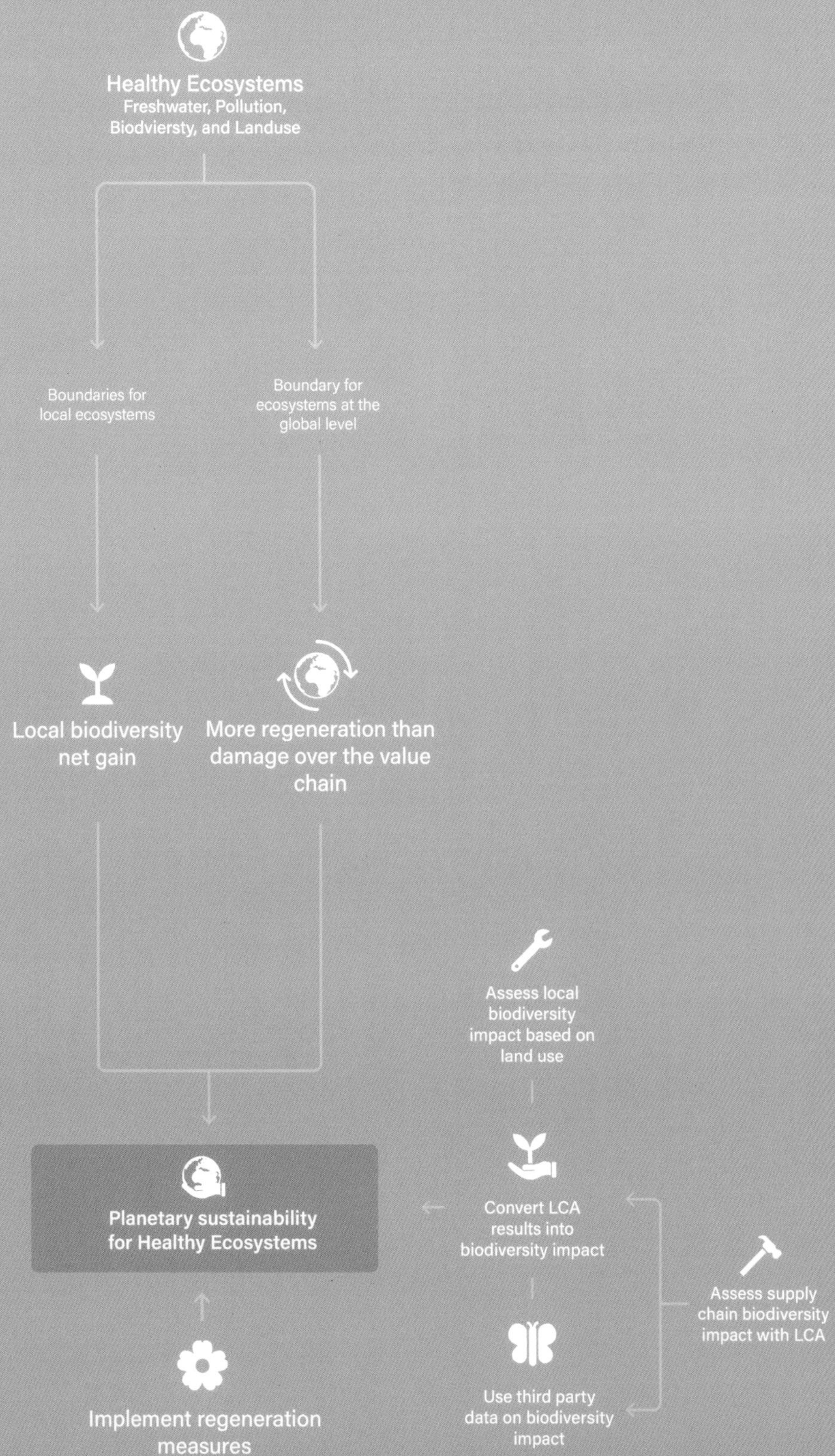

Healthy Ecosystems
Freshwater, Pollution, Biodviersty, and Landuse
Boundaries for local ecosystems
Boundary for ecosystems at the global level
Local biodiversity net gain
More regeneration than damage over the value chain
Assess local biodiversity impact based on land use
Planetary sustainability for Healthy Ecosystems
Convert LCA results into biodiversity impact
Assess supply chain biodiversity impact with LCA
Use third party data on biodiversity impact
Implement regeneration measures

Healthy Ecosystems

Healthy ecosystems are assessed through several related but distinct aspects. First, **biodiversity loss** directly measures the health and diversity of species in an ecosystem. **Biodiversity loss** is measured by two factors; genetic diversity and functional diversity.

Genetic diversity is important for species and population survival, evolution and adaptation to future conditions. Genetic diversity is estimated with the global control variable "number of extinct species per 1000 years". The reference Holocene scenario is <2-3 species extinctions per 1000 years, whereas the current global estimate is 100-1000 species per 1000 years (hence why the current period is called the 6th mass extinction).

Functional diversity represents the role of the biosphere in regulating other Earth-system processes. It is estimated with two control variables: **Biodiversity Intactness Index** (**BII**) and **Human appropriated net primary production** (**HANPP**). The BII is an estimated percentage of the original number of species that remain and their abundance in any given area, despite land use change and other human pressures. HANPP is a measure of human alterations of photosynthetic production and the harvest of products of photosynthesis. Photosynthetic production determines the energy available for transfer from plants to other organisms. Alteration of this flow influences biodiversity as well as water flow, carbon flow and thus other planetary boundaries (Haberl et al. 2007).

Additionally, **land use change** is essential to understand healthy ecosystems. In the planetary boundaries framework, the control variable for land use change is the amount of tropical, temperate and boreal forest cover remaining (Steffen et al. 2015). As such, the land use change control variable is not in itself a comprehensive measure of healthy ecosystems, since it focuses only on forests and their role in climate regulation. However, land use change is a major driver in ecosystem damage for all types of ecosystems.

The availability of **freshwater** is highly important for healthy ecosystems. Freshwater withdrawal influences the amount of water available for natural ecosystems and populations, and excessive withdrawal may alter entire ecosystems. Transgressing the freshwater boundary also poses a risk to human populations since this essential resource is used at a rate which is higher than the ability of the water system to regenerate, leading to water deficiency in the long run.

Two parameters are used for freshwater. The first is the consumption and withdrawal of "blue water" from rivers, lakes, reservoirs, and renewable groundwater stores (Steffen et al. 2015). The second is "green water", covering terrestrial precipitation, evaporation, and soil moisture (Wang-Erlandsson et al., 2022).

Finally, it is important to monitor pollutants which may spread into the environment, accumulate and cause environmental degradation of the Earth system. Three planetary boundaries deal with such pollutants: **aerosols** (which affect human health and the climate), **novel entities** (which create risks of long-lasting negative effects) and **nitrogen** and **phosphorous flows** (which cause eutrophication). In general, we measure either the volume of produced pollutant, the concentration of the pollutant in the environment, or the actual effects of the pollutant. The closer to the site of production, the easier to measure direct impact, but the larger the uncertainty of the correlation with actual, indirect impacts (Persson et al., 2022).

Planetary positive on-site

The impacts of urban development on healthy ecosystems can be split into local impacts occurring on and around the development site, and remote impacts occurring throughout the global supply chain, linked for instance with the production of construction materials. Local impacts are easier to understand and measure, because they can be made visible to the developer, project teams and stakeholders. Because of the local scale and smaller geographical distribution, on-site impacts can often be measured directly by surveys and mapping of projected ecosystem change, freshwater use etc. However, some of the control variables mentioned above are difficult to scale down, and other indicators might be more appropriate for decision support at the local level.

To assess impacts on **biodiversity loss** and **land use change**, a dedicated biodiversity metric developed for the UK planning legislation can be used (Natural England, 2023). The tool has been integrated into BREEAM Schemes for sustainability assessment, and in Denmark the methodology is currently being developed as a national survey method for urban nature. The 'Biodiversity Net Gain' approach compares the types of land and habitats in the area before the project, in the project plans, and after the project is realised. See "How do you define a project's biodiversity baseline?" on the next spread.

Different areas are attributed different values representing their importance for biodiversity, based on the type of habitat (woodland, grassland, bare ground, etc.), its distinguishing features, its condition (quality and health of the habitat), and its strategic significance for biodiversity in the surrounding area. Based on these values, each area is attributed a score representing its importance for biodiversity. The tool calculates the total biodiversity impact of the project and of any regenerative measure by comparing the biodiversity values of all areas before and after development. The results can be used to document the project's impact on **biodiversity loss** and **land use change** on-site, and find ways of reducing negative impacts. It can also help identify opportunities to regenerate biodiversity in vulnerable areas, with the aim to provide a positive value that outweighs the project's residual negative impacts in vulnerable areas off-site. More details are provided in the Appendix Chapter 4 and Chapter 7.

To assess impacts on freshwater and the release of pollutants, multiple indicators should be reported. This includes indicators for freshwater use and amount of infiltration (which affects groundwater levels as well as lakes and rivers). Pollutants can be tracked via indicators for the number of pollutants used in the development and potentially leaching from the development site, as well as indicators related to waste handling (to minimise the risk of pollutants such as plastics spreading to the environment). Protocols and detailed criteria to monitor these aspects are already implemented in sustainability assessments for certifications such as DGNB or BREEAM.

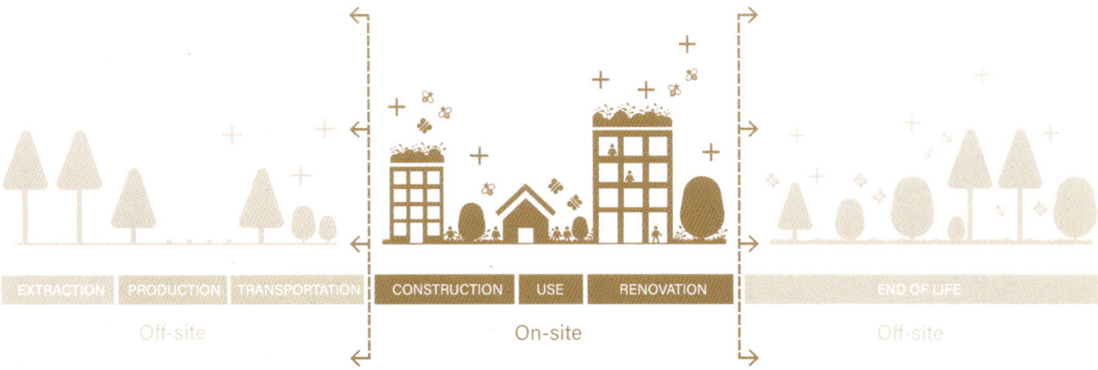

Figure 29: In business-as-usual scenarios biodiversity is considered an on-site (local) issue, but if we're to truly apply Doughnut principles in urban development we must apply a life-cycle perspective which includes the quantification of off-site (global) biodiversity impacts that happen across the supply chain. We can measure biodiversity on-site (locally) with the 'Biodiversity Net Gain' method and biodiversity impact off-site (globally) can be done using the 'Off-site Biodiversity Tool'

How do you define a project's biodiversity baseline?

The Planetary Boundaries framework assesses the state of boundaries compared to a baseline, set either at pre-industrial times or at the start of the Holocene (roughly 9,000 years BCE). The point is to show the impacts caused by human activity on the various boundaries.

For climate change, it is possible to define and aim for a boundary based on atmospheric concentration of carbon to preserve the climate conditions of the Holocene. However, ecosystems are fundamentally different: it is nearly impossible to revert to a Holocene-like state, since lost species cannot be brought back and converted ecosystems cannot be restored back to pristine conditions. Therefore, to document the effects of human activity for a specific development, the chosen baseline is often the state of the development area prior to the development. In most cases, that implies considering previous land use, which may be urban, industrial, agricultural or natural ecosystems. The baseline is thereby not determined by the ownership or planning status of an area, but by the physical and ecological quality.

Ecosystem impacts over the entire supply chain

Both the local and the global dimensions of healthy ecosystems are important to achieve planetary sustainability. In fact, impacts on ecosystems happening far up the supply chain of the project are sometimes much larger than local impacts. For instance, a large part of the impact from urban development happens far from the development site due to the extraction of river sand for concrete production or forestry activities for timber production. It is therefore crucial to consider impacts on ecosystems over the entire life cycle, and to avoid the pitfall of improving local biodiversity at the expense of other ecosystems far from the project location.

LCA is used to assess environmental impacts over the full life cycle. Some common building LCA tools and databases (such as Ökobaudat, n.d.9) include valuable information to assess life cycle impacts related to freshwater use and pollutants. The life cycle indicators "net freshwater use", "hazardous waste disposed", "radioactive waste disposed", "eutrophication potential" and "acidification potential" reported in the EN 15804+A2 norm are particularly relevant. This norm also includes an indicator for soil quality, which can be used to assess impacts on land use. However, the indicator is still quite new as of 2023, with limited data available. In the coming years, we can hope to see an increase in data availability for all these indicators, through generic LCA databases and published Environmental Product Declarations (EPDs).

When it comes to **biodiversity loss** most freely available building LCA tools and databases do not include impact categories corresponding to genetic or functional diversity. A direct of an assessment as for climate change, is therefore impossible. However, it is possible to calculate impacts on biodiversity over the entire value chain using more detailed LCA tools and data. For instance, programs like SimaPro and OpenLCA can be used to calculate impacts on human health, ecosystems, and natural resources (so-called "endpoint" impact categories). Similarly, LCA databases like Ecoinvent and Sphera/GaBi for example, include environmental data for a range of generic products. Selecting data using the 'ReCiPe 2016 endpoint' method in these databases will provide information on impacts on biodiversity loss for all products (in species.year). Furthermore, these databases include data on land use as well as other relevant indicators for functioning ecosystems mentioned above. However, these databases are not freely available, and require an investment both in time and money.

The 'Off-site Biodiversity Tool' was developed for the Doughnut for Urban Development to simplify calculations of impacts on biodiversity loss over the full life cycle. It is freely available, but relies on third-party data that cannot be made publicly available for licensing reasons. Users will need to purchase a license to an appropriate third-party environmental database, and plug in the data into the spreadsheet tool themselves. Alternatively, users can convert LCA results from other LCA tools into impacts on biodiversity, provided that the converted results include all important impact categories, including land use and ecotoxicity.

The tool calculates both on-site biodiversity impacts (from local land use) and life-cycle impacts from the use of materials, measured in species.year. The on-site impacts related to land use are included and expressed in the same unit as impacts from material use, for the purpose of comparison and comprehensiveness. However, the on-site assessment in this tool is much coarser than with the biodiversity metric described in the previous section – it is therefore not a substitute for the biodiversity metric, but a complement. The 'Off-site Biodiversity Tool' can be found in the Appendix Chapter 4 and Chapter 7.

Both the local and the global dimensions of healthy ecosystems are important to achieve planetary sustainability.
In fact, impacts on ecosystems happening far up the supply chain of the project are sometimes much larger than local impacts. It is therefore crucial to consider impacts on ecosystems over the entire life cycle, and to avoid the pitfall of improving local biodiversity at the expense of other ecosystems far from the project location.

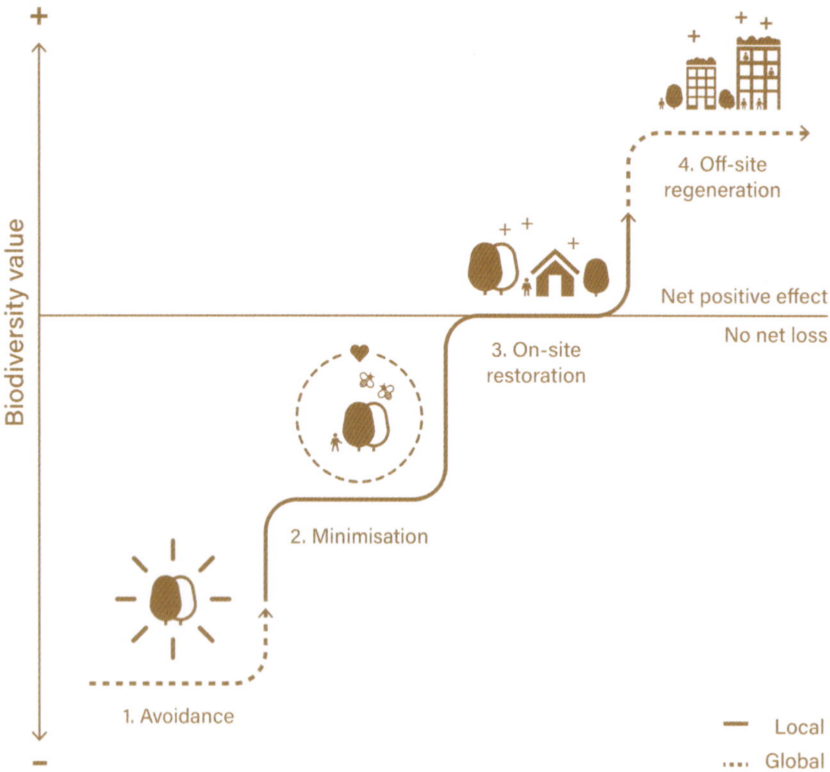

Figure 30: This figure illustrates the 'Biodiversity Net Gain' mitigation hierarchy. Where avoidance, minimisation, on-site restoration, and off-site regeneration steer urban development towards biodiversity net gain (Original illustration inspired by SLA).

From degenerative to regenerative

This section addresses the importance of mitigation and regeneration measures and their differences, to ensure that the development lives up to the regenerative aspirations of Doughnut Economics. Having identified the development's impacts on ecosystems and the climate, developers should follow the mitigation hierarchy when implementing measures to reach the targets:

1. Avoidance
First, damaging activities should be avoided whenever possible.

2. Minimisation
When such activities cannot be avoided, their impact should be minimised.

3. On-site restoration
Remaining damage should be re-mediated through measures taken within the development area (such as establishing new habitats within the area)

4. Off-site regeneration
Finally, the development should contribute to regeneration along each of the environmental aspects it affects. Ideally, regenerative activities should be performed as close as possible to the affected areas, but regeneration might sometimes require investing in other areas.

This priority order is crucial to be consistent with Doughnut Economics. It is essential to first address the root causes of environmental damage and minimise this damage. However, to achieve very ambitious sustainability targets and to be truly transformative, mitigating negative impacts is not enough: it is important for the project to create positive impacts through regeneration within and beyond the physical boundaries of the project area.

The Doughnut principles require shifting the way we think about the project's impacts. The focus is not just on reducing negative impacts on-site - rather, positivity becomes a core value, and the question "How can the project contribute to regenerating the Earth system, both locally and globally?" becomes an essential goal.

Notably, regeneration strives to create positive environmental impacts that can match or surpass those provided by ecosystem services from native habitats. To emphasize this shift, it is important to consider regeneration ("how to do more good") separately from mitigation ("how to do less bad"). The two concepts are essential but fundamentally different components of planetary sustainability. This means for instance that positive impacts from regenerative practices should never simply be subtracted from the project's negative impacts, but reported separately.

In the same vein, we deliberately avoid the terms "compensation" or "offsetting" used in other frameworks (such as the Science-Based Targets Initiative or several net-zero building standards). These terms evoke the idea of making up for something bad.

Conversely, regeneration emphasises two important ideas:
1. Negative impacts cannot always be compensated (damaging one area and restoring another is not a neutral outcome for biodiversity or local populations), and

2. We should strive for positive impacts not just to make up for negative impacts, but because they are essential in themselves.

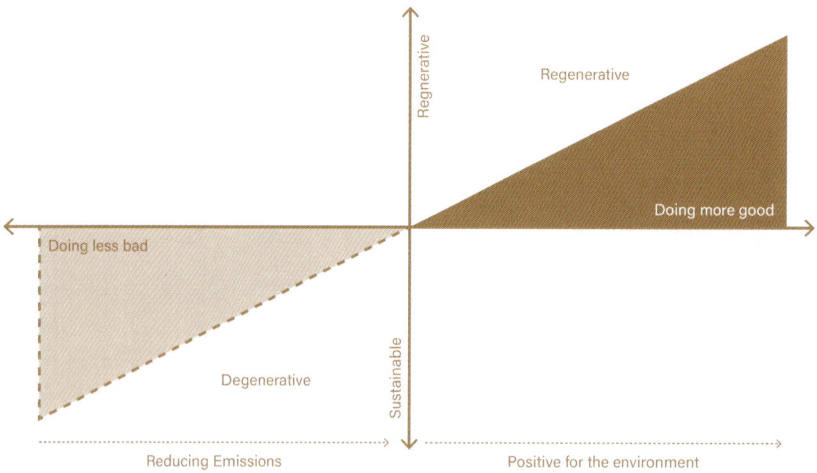

Figure 31: From degenerative "doing less bad" and reducing emissions to regenerative "doing more good" or creating positive impact for the environment. Illustration adopted from Bill Reed.

With this distinction in mind, every planetary sustainability target can be thought of as two sub-targets:

- A target for mitigation: reduce the project's negative impacts as much as best practice allows.
- A target for regeneration: create positive environmental impacts that match or surpass those provided by ecosystem services from native habitats, and that outweigh the residual negative impacts.

Regeneration linked with healthy ecosystems

Regenerative activities must follow important quality criteria to ensure that they reliably provide positive impacts (Broekhoff et al., 2019) **Figure 31**:

- **Measurability**: The regenerative benefits should be possible to assess with robust data and methods, including both direct and indirect impacts.
- **Additionality:** Are we confident that the environmental benefits would not happen if the regenerative activity was not carried out? For instance, you can't claim benefits from preserving a forest if the forest was not at a high risk of being cut down in the first place.
- **Permanence:** Benefits that are likely to persist for a long time in the future should be prioritised.
- **Exclusivity:** It is important to ensure that no other actor is claiming the benefits of a given activity, to avoid double-counting.
- **Positive impacts:** Regenerative activities must never cause significant damage to other environmental categories. Regeneration should not harm any population, and strive for positive social impacts as well (a counter-example is the appropriation of land in low-income countries for carbon offsets).

For climate change, mitigation would entail reducing the project's life cycle climate impact to match best practice in the country. Regeneration would entail removing greenhouse gases from the atmosphere or avoiding greenhouse gas emissions in order to reach the allocated climate targets described earlier in this chapter.

This includes in particular:

- Producing low-carbon electricity in excess of the building's needs (for instance using rooftop PV panels) and exporting it to the grid to replace more polluting electricity sources.
- Designing the building specifically to facilitate disassembly and the reuse of construction products in the future.
- Investing in carbon-removal activities on- or off-site.

The latter can entail investing in "carbon offsets", with sufficient quality control to ensure that they fulfil the quality criteria mentioned above. Some examples include: forestation, storing carbon in the soil, coastal blue carbon, storing carbon through enhanced weathering, direct air capture and storage of carbon (DACCS) (Klimate.co; offsetguide.org) and are described in **Figure 33**.

Independent programmes such as VERRA, Gold Standard or Plan Vivo offer some level of quality control for these offsets (for instance ensuring exclusivity criteria). However, many offsets from these programmes (in particular related to forestation) have been criticised for being unreliable or disrespecting local populations. It is therefore recommended to conduct further investigation into the quality of carbon removal initiatives (Broekhoff et al., 2019).

More details on how to account for these various activities and how to quantify the related climate benefits (to be reported separately) can be found in Appendix Chapter 5.

For biodiversity, mitigation entails avoiding or minimising the project's impact on local ecosystems,

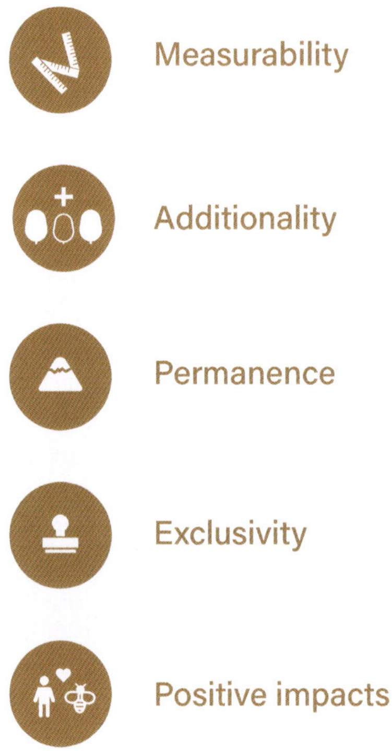

Figure 32: Regenerative activities must follow important quality criteria to ensure that they reliably provide positive impacts (Broekhoff et al., 2019).

as well as the life-cycle impact on other ecosystems, as much as possible.

Regeneration takes different forms for local and global impacts. Locally, ecosystems in and around the project area can be restored in order to improve biodiversity, following the local 'Biodiversity Net Gain' approach highlighted earlier in this section. This can for instance entail planting trees or wild flowers on the project area, or providing habitats for local birds and insects.

Regenerating biodiversity throughout the project's entire supply chain is more complicated. It is very difficult for a development project to contribute directly to restoration activities in each ecosystem affected, for example by the extraction of natural resources to produce building materials. Unexamined biodiversity offsets risk causing land appropriation and "license to trash", where damaging projects are enabled by promises of restoration that are unreliable or disrespectful of local populations (Hahn et al., 2022).

Biocredits

Recently, "biocredits" have been proposed as a regulated way for actors to support ecosystem restoration by local communities and indigenous people in other countries (Ducros & Steele, 2022).

Biocredits are generated by indigenous people and local communities that preserve existing ecosystems or regenerate damaged ecosystems. This can for instance include forestation initiatives driven by indigenous people, but also community-driven conservancies in threatened areas. They can then be purchased by individuals and companies all around the world, to finance further conservation efforts from local communities. A very important difference between biocredits and carbon offsets is that biocredits explicitly cannot be used for claims of offsetting – they promote regeneration, but do not compensate for negative impacts.

Biocredits are not yet a mature solution, but organisations such as Terrasos, Wallacea Trust and ValueNature already provide biocredit schemes. They represent a promising way forward to support regeneration remotely. Overall, developers might be able to support ecosystem restoration remotely by investing in biocredits or individual restoration projects, but they should not claim that this compensates for a project's negative impacts.

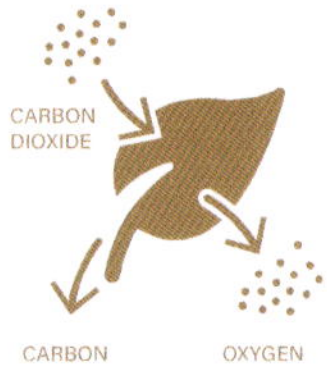

Forestation
Forestation is simply the process of planting trees in areas affected by deforestation, desertification, or as part of agroforestry. Compared to the other examples, forestation scores lower on criteria of permanence, since it does not guarantee that carbon will be stored in the long term. However, if done well it can provide many co-benefits – including for biodiversity.

Soil
This can be done by mixing in biochar, a residue from the pyrolysis of organic matter. The production of biochar produces oils and gases that can be used for energy recovery. Biochar can be added to soil, where it can improve soil fertility, or to building materials such as concrete (as a partial substitute for cement). Its benefits are highly dependent on its stability and the amount of biomass needed for its production (Azzi, 2021; Fawzy et al., 2021).

Costal blue carbon
Coastal ecosystems such as mangroves, salt marshes, and sea grasses, have the ability to capture and store carbon dioxide from the atmosphere. These ecosystems absorb carbon dioxide through photosynthesis and sequester it in their plants and sediments. Restoring coastal ecosystems helps to mitigate climate change by reducing greenhouse gas emissions and works to protect fragile coastlines while enhancing biodiversity.

Enhanced weathering
Silicate minerals are ground into small pieces. Silicate minerals have a natural ability to absorb CO2. Grinding them into small particles considerably increases the surface in contact with the air, speeding up the process. Using these minerals in agriculture can lead to healthier soils, while spreading them on beaches can help combat ocean acidification (Hartmann et al., 2013).

Direct air capture (DACCS)
Direct air capture and storage of CO_2 (DACCS) uses large fan-like devices to remove CO_2 from the air and store it (usually underground). The first large-scale DACCS plant was opened in Iceland in 2021. DACCS could become a major carbon removal technology, although some economic and technical challenges (e.g. related to energy use) remain to be addressed (Breyer et al., 2019; Fasihi et al., 2019).

Quality control
It is important to underline that not all carbon mitigation activities are created equal and life cycle thinking should be applied when working to mitigate carbon impacts. Work with reputable programs such as VERRA, Gold Standard or Plan Vivo, while conducting independent investigation into the quality of carbon removal initiatives

Figure 33: Regenerative activities must follow important quality criteria to ensure that they reliably provide positive impacts (Broekhoff et al., 2019).

The focus is not just on reducing negative impacts - rather, positivity becomes a core value, and the question “How can the project contribute to regenerating the Earth system, both locally and globally?” becomes an essential goal.

Doughnut Design for Business

05

In this chapter we introduce and detail the 'Doughnut Design for Business' tool, which works to transform business towards regenerative ends through deep design.

In this chapter, we introduce the idea that for a business to pursue regenerative outcomes it should also look inward on its business design. As a framework for this exploration, we introduce the 'Doughnut Design for Business' tool (DEAL, 2022). This tool emphasises five crucial "deep design" aspects that organisations need to consider in order to effectively pursue regenerative and distributive outcomes aligned with the principles of Doughnut Economics.

These aspects, namely Purpose, Networks, Governance, Ownership, and Finance, serve as fundamental building blocks for businesses to create a positive impact on both the environment and society.

To illustrate the application of these deep design aspects, a case study on Home.Earth is included in the chapter. This case study showcases how Home.Earth, a company in the real estate sector, embraces various elements of business design to pursue regenerative outcomes in urban development and address systemic challenges within the industry. Tangible examples demonstrate how integrating deep design principles can lead to transformative and sustainable business practices.

Deep Design of Businesses

The 21st century's rapidly compounding crises – from climate and ecological breakdown to extreme social inequities of power and opportunity – make it irrefutably clear that the global economic system must be transformed if humanity and the rest of life on Earth are to thrive.

Doughnut Economics provides an increasingly recognised compass for such a thriving future, and is focused on meeting the needs of all people within the means of the living planet, by creating economies that are regenerative and distributive by design. What are the implications for the role and transformation of business, if it is to be part of this future?

Getting into the Doughnut calls for nothing less than a transformation in the dynamics of the global economy. Today's degenerative industrial systems – inherited from the last century – are still using up and running down the living world, and must rapidly be turned into regenerative industries that work with Earth's cycles and within Earth's means. At the same time, today's divisive context – thanks to the concentration of ownership and power in far too few hands – must be turned into distributive outcomes, through an economy that shares value and opportunity far more equitably with all who co-create it. What, then, does Doughnut Economics mean for business?

It calls on businesses to demonstrate how they are going to transform so that they will belong in this future – aligned to, and in service of, a world where all people and the living planet thrive. For many companies, moving towards such a transformation typically begins with innovations in product design, eliminating single-use plastics and built-in obsolescence, while committing to paying living wages for the supply-chain workers making the products.

Such actions are an important start, but they are far from sufficient if business is to become not just 'more sustainable' but regenerative by design, and not just 'more inclusive' but distributive by design. Reaching this scale of ambition calls for transforming not only the design of products, but the deep design of business itself. As described by Marjorie Kelly, a leading theorist in next-generation enterprise design, there are five key layers of design that powerfully shape what an organisation can do and be in the world: Purpose. Networks. Governance. Ownership. Finance, as illustrated by **Figure 34.**

Together these five aspects of organisational design profoundly shape any organisation's ability to become regenerative and distributive by design, and so help bring humanity into the Doughnut.

Innovations in the five layers of business design – through Purpose, Networks, Governance, Ownership, and Finance – are essential if business is to become regenerative and distributive in its strategies, operations, and impacts, thereby helping to bring humanity into the Doughnut.

Doughnut Economics is, of course, far from the only initiative calling for business transformation. Many other initiatives and approaches are already underway, with many different points of focus: shifting the mindset of business leaders; promoting consumer and investor action; supporting collective action by workers, farmers, and communities; promoting democratisation of business; and developing impact measurement to set better targets for businesses. Governments have likewise introduced rules and regulations, taxes, subsidies, new alliances, and innovation programmes intended to promote sustainable and social business practices, such as through ESG (environmental, social, and governance) reporting, carbon pricing, and extended producer responsibility. These are all important contributions to achieving the change needed in the business world but, as this paper argues, the transformative change required will only be achieved by also transforming the deep design of business itself. Deep design focuses on the ownership and financial structure of an enterprise; how it manages relationships with suppliers, clients, and stakeholders; how it makes and monitors key decisions; and how it sets and protects its purpose. In this sense, enterprise (re)design is foundational for many other transformations, in both business and the wider economy, that can help to bring humanity within the safe and just space of the Doughnut.

Focusing on deep design is a fast-evolving approach to transforming business. New design innovations necessary for business to become regenerative and distributive are now being created and explored; already the scope of what may be possible is emerging.

From a regenerative perspective, for example, consider business designs that make Earth the sole shareholder, a board director, or the chief executive of a company. Examples like this already exist: U.S. outdoor clothing company Patagonia has made Earth its "only shareholder"U.K. based shampoo company Faith In Nature has "appointed Nature to its board" and Willicroft, a Dutch plant-based cheese company, has shaped the chief executive role to ensure that Nature is the priority. Design innovations like these can fundamentally affect the likelihood of a business taking transformative regenerative action, for instance by giving the green light to a regenerative agriculture proposal, making significant investments in carbon-positive construction, or achieving beyond a living wage for supply chain workers. While the counter-factual outcome – "What would have happened without that particular business design?" – Is hard to determine, the deep design of a business is certainly a pivotal factor in shaping its key strategies, decisions and actions.

From a distributive perspective, consider the transformative actions that can be pursued when the interests of the people most connected to, or impacted by, a business are core to its deep design. Examples exist, such as wool and fashion producers Manos del Uruguay, whose profits are always used to generate benefits for its artisans across rural Uruguay. Consider Amul, a dairy company in India whose small-scale farmers own the business, thus benefiting both from its profits and from having purchasing practices designed to support their needs. Likewise consider the rise of affordable community-owned renewable energy suppliers, such as the 1,900 citizen-led energy cooperatives in the REScoop Federation, representing over 1.25 million people across Europe.

While none of these businesses would yet claim to be fully regenerative and distributive by design, they collectively demonstrate that innovations in the deep design of business – its Purpose, Networks, Governance, Ownership, and Finance – can unlock transformative action to open up far greater scope for business to become part of a regenerative and distributive future.

DESIGN LAYER	SUMMARY	EXAMPLES OF DESIGN IN PRACTICE
Purpose	The purpose of a business is the fundamental reason why it exists. It is not only found in a company's words but in it's culture and operations, and across it's core products and services. It is reinforced by the broader design of the business.	• Mission-look through a social enterprise structure. • The stated social and / or ecological purpose is embedded through other layers of the design.
Networks	Businesses create and belong to multiple networks. This includes trading networks across their supply chains, networks with commercial partners, and networks with their staff, customers and governments. Businesses also belong to networks of peers in their industry and broader association.	• Long-term and committed partnerships with suppliers. • Long-term commitment to staff, upholding all labour rights. • Part of progressive business networks.
Governance	The governance structure of a business determines how decisions are made. This covers who is represented on the board, how trade-offs are navigated, transparency of the business, what information and metrics are included in annual accounts, and the use of internal incentives to pursue the company's purpose.	• Mutli-stakeholder representation on the board. • Mission-lock through an NGO or purpose foundation holding veto power.
Ownership	Who owns the business, and to what extent can these owners change or undermine its intended purpose? Deciding which stakeholders are represented in the ownership mix, and the expectations of owners on ecological, social, and financial performance, can be pivotal.	• Mutli-stakeholder representation on the board. •Mission-lock through an NGO or purpose foundation holding veto power.
Finance	The relationship with finance is a key determinant of a business's ability to become regenerative and distributive. Margin requirements, dividend expectations, and internal reinvestments (capital expenditure) and profit allocation rules are a key part of this. To shape financial parameters so as to enable transformative ideas, the question of a fair return for investors will also arise.	• Flexible margins for positive impact ideas. • Dividends cap to enable internal investments in regenerative ideas.

Regenerative and distributive business dynamics
Working with Doughnut Economics helps businesses to understand the scale of transformation that is needed. The global economy is overshooting Earth's capacity to support life, while billions of people are still falling short on life's essentials. For humanity to thrive, it is essential to move into the doughnut-shaped space between the ecological ceiling and the social foundation by creating a regenerative and distributive economy. The implications for business are profound, requiring two major transformations.

The deep design of business
The application of Doughnut Economics to business focuses on transforming the deep design of business. By deep design we mean the purpose of the business, how it operates in networks, how it is governed, how it is owned, and the nature of its relationship with finance. The deep design of business is crucial for the creation and implementation of the transformative regenerative and distributive actions which are required to get humanity into the Doughnut.

The five layers of business design
In order to explore the layers of the deep design of business, we have taken inspiration from the work of author and thought leader Marjorie Kelly. In particular, Doughnut Economics has drawn from Kelly's five "design elements of enterprise ownership". Doughnut Economics summarises these as Purpose, Networks, Governance, Ownership, and Finance.

Focusing on deep design is a fast-evolving approach to transforming business.
New design innovations necessary for business to become regenerative and are now being created and explored; already the scope of what may be possible is emerging.

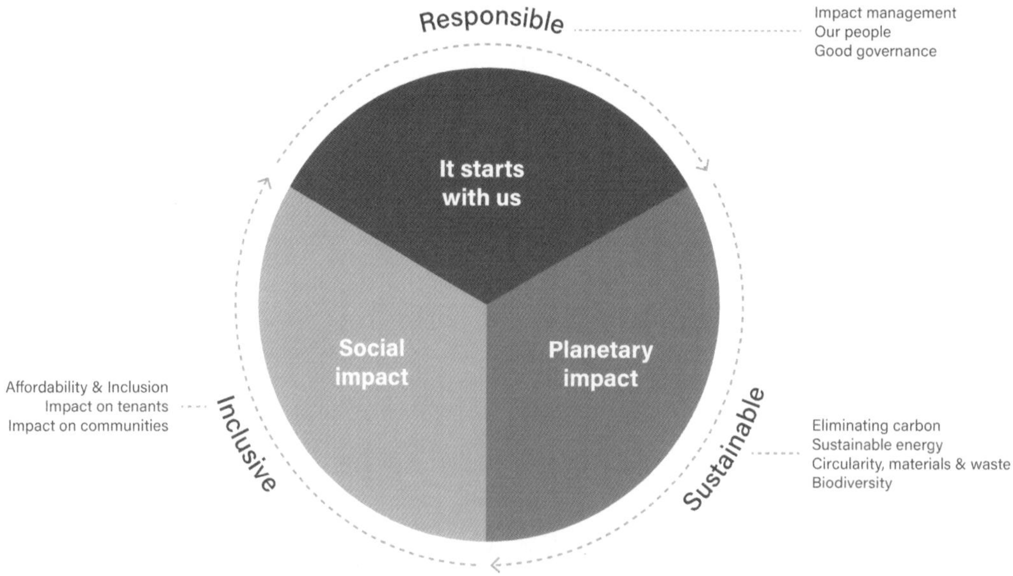

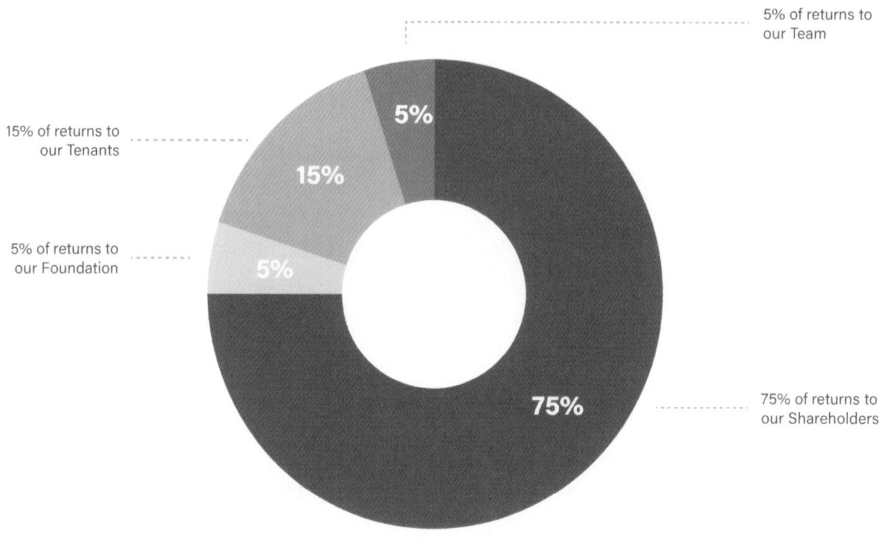

Figure 35: Home.Earth's guiding principles and economic structure for urban development.

Regenerative urban development company

Real estate and the urban environment have a profound impact on all of us. We spend 90% of our lives inside buildings. And by 2050 almost 70% of us will live in cities. The built environment enables life, community and culture. But at the same time, it fosters loneliness and health issues. It counts for almost 40% of global CO_2 emissions. It is the biggest living expense for most people. And nowhere is growing inequality more visible than in how we live.

To overcome the challenges, the business design of the companies operating in the urban space must be revisited, moving from short-term profit maximisation to long-lasting holistic value creation. Home.Earth has set out to be a pathfinder on this journey and has developed a business design and stakeholder-anchored governance model, which they hope can serve as inspiration for other companies on a similar journey.

Introducing Home.Earth

Home.Earth is an urban development company founded in the beginning of 2021 by a diverse team of experienced leaders from real estate, investments, architecture, sustainability, and social entrepreneurship. As an integrated investor, developer and housing operator, Home.Earth will be designing, building, and operating homes and spaces - initially in Copenhagen, but with European ambitions.
Inspired by Doughnut Economics, Home.Earth approach their purpose with a holistic definition of "people and planet positive" and an ultimate aim of being a regenerative company. As such, Home.Earth is using the planetary boundaries as the guiding framework for their ecological impacts while they optimise for, e.g., affordability, liveability, inclusive, and a responsible supply chain within their social impact, drawing on the 12 social dimensions from the Doughnut.

The ambitions are about to come to life in Home. Earth's first development project in Copenhagen, where they will create ~150 homes and ~2,000 m2 of active commercial space, starting construction in early 2023.

Structural challenges in the real estate sector

Two core challenges are hampering the real estate sector from contributing to solving the challenges our cities are facing. First, the real estate sector is held back by a fragmented value chain, causing the sector to optimise for the short-term instead of the long-term. In a classic development project, most actors - such as the architect, the engineer, the developer and the contractor - are only involved in 2-5 years and thus take decisions that optimise value creation within those 2-5 years and often primarily from a financial perspective for themselves. But given buildings and the communities in and around the buildings live for 50 to 100 years - if not longer - it is critical that decisions are made to optimise long-term value creation and life-cycle cost. We need to better incentivise all actors to optimise for the long term, even if it costs in the short term.

The other core challenge in real estate today is that the development and operation of real estate is driven by the interests of the developer/investor/owner/landlord rather than other key stakeholders such as tenants, communities, and our planet. While investors should receive a fair return and appropriate levels of governance rights and protection, it is necessary to distribute influence to other stakeholders as well to align interests and enable maximum value creation across multiple bottom lines.

Rethinking business design to build a regenerative urban real estate company

Home.Earth fully believes the right business design is fundamental to not only enable and support but also safeguard long-lasting positive impact. For this reason, Home.Earth has taken a number of steps in its business design to achieve this, with these key elements:

1. Purpose, values and culture
2. Intentionality, measurement and transparency
3. Stakeholder anchored governance model
4. Mission-lock through the Home.Earth Foundation
5. Sharing of value creation among all key stakeholders

While the first point above in principle applies to all companies, Home.Earth highlights the importance of it and therefore its included here. Home.Earth believe the second point will increasingly apply to business and Home.Earth desires to be a leader in terms of impact management. The last 3 points are the core elements where Home.Earth demonstrates a new business design and hence these three points are the most important and where Home.Earth is truly different. Altogether the 5 elements listed above aligns well with the five organisational design aspects from the Doughnut Design for Businesses tool.

1. Purpose, values and culture:

Home.Earth believes in operating according to a purpose that is meaningful for all stakeholders is fundamental. The purpose must be supported by clear and strong values, which in the case of Home.Earth are: courage, trust, care and integrity. Together the purpose and values will enable the company culture that can enable the desired performance and impact. Home.Earth has chosen to organize according to Holacracy as they believe this help enable the purpose, values and culture.

2. Intentionality, measurement and transparency by design

Figure 33a illustrates the three dimensions of the impact management framework that Home.Earth has designed and adopted. Home.Earth is embedding impact criteria in all its core processes and decisions. This entails for example that social and planetary impact targets are conditions for investments and operations. Home.Earth has also integrated business design and good governance principles into the core of their impact management framework. Alongside social impact and planetary impact, the third area in their impact management framework is titled "It starts with us". In other words, Home.Earth will measure its success and failures within regenerative business design. This includes, for example, measuring the degree of supply chain transparency, the amount of value created for tenants, and the diversity of its board.

3. A truly stakeholder anchored governance model

Home.Earth believe that if we truly want to move to a stakeholder based economy, then this will only be feasible if we also move from shareholder control to stakeholder governance. Home.Earth has implemented a governance model where key stakeholders all have representation and influence, but where no single stakeholder ultimately controls the company. Single stakeholders have veto rights on topics of particular importance to them, but the objective has to balance governance appropriately for the long-term interests of all stakeholders. For shareholders specifically, they have representation at all the various levels in the governance structure and they have veto on a number of elements that are deemed of key importance to them, so shareholders are very involved in the governance of Home.Earth, but they do not have positive control of the company.

Case Study. Nærheden, Copenhagen. Developer, Home.Earth. Architect, Vandkunsten, EFFEKT. Landscape, Vandkunsten, SLA. Year 2024. Size, 13.500 m2

4. Mission-lock through the Home.Earth Foundation

As a purpose-guided company and the desire to safeguard the purpose long-term, Home.Earth has found a way to create "mission-lock" with an established foundation controlling the purpose of the company. The structure draws on the success of many Danish companies, such as Lego, Maersk, Novo Nordisk and Carlsberg, that have established foundations that control the relevant companies. The Danish foundation structure ensure that the objective or purpose of the company cannot be changed and that the company operates for the long-term.

In the case of Home.Earth, the Foundation does not control the company given the stakeholder governance model outlined above. However, the Foundation control the Purpose of Home.Earth in that the foundation has veto-right on any decision that relates to the Purpose of the company. In practice the Foundation hold 35% of the voting rights in the company and besides the role in relation to the Purpose, then the foundation also holds a key role in regards to ensuring quality and stakeholder representation in the Board of Home.Earth

5. Sharing of value creation among all key stakeholders

In societies across the world the gap between rich and poor is growing. Among the winners are those with capital as well as those that manage the capital. In real estate this problem is particularly pronounced - real estate is the largest investment asset class in the world and it has delivered strong and resilient returns over very long periods of time - however at the same time, there are a places where inequality is more present than in how people live given that it is the largest living expense for most people.

Home.Earth has implemented a stakeholder model in relation to value creation and sharing of this value that can be seen in **Figure 33b**. The majority of the financial return still accrues to investors (75%), but there is also an allocation to the tenants of the company (15%), to the Home.Earth team (5%) and to society through the Foundation (5%). This enable a unique dynamic where all key stakeholders have the same financial incentives to maximise value creation in Home.Earth, which they believe will ultimately benefit shareholders also. The sharing of value is a straight split (i.e. no "hurdle rates" or similar) that enable full alignment at all times, which is also seen as relative to traditional financial models.

For tenants it means that living with Home.Earth is a hybrid between owning and renting in the traditional sense. To tackle urban economic inequality, Home.Earth is treating all its tenants as co-owners of the company - and the 15% of the company's financial return shared with tenants translates to roughly 20-25% of rent paid over time in a normal economic environment and hence should enable a stable, affordable, and attractive housing option for tenants. This will, over time, hopefully translate to access to home ownership for tenants that cannot otherwise build enough savings to buy their own home. Alongside recognising tenants for the value they bring, Home.Earth believe that this hybrid model of ownership will lead to tenants feeling and acting as owners rather than tenants, to the benefit of both tenants, landlord/shareholders and our planet.

As a final note - Home.Earth highlights that while Home.Earth believe rethinking business design is essential from a planet and people perspective, then Home.Earth also believe that rethinking business design can drive better financial performance and profit. Home.Earth is convinced that being intentional about purpose and impact, aligning stakeholders, creating mission-lock to force long-term thinking will benefit shareholders as much as people and planet.

Our purpose: change real estate to serve the whole. We develop inclusive and sustainable urban communities designed to enhance life that demonstrate a path towards an equitable and responsible business paradigm.

References & Credits

06

References

Books, research papers, journals, reports

Arup. (2021). Designing for planetary boundary cities. Arup. https://www.arup.com/perspectives/publications/research/section/planetary-boundaries

Azzi, E. (2021). Biochar systems across scales in Sweden: An industrial ecology perspective. PhD thesis, KTH Royal Institute of Technology. https://www.diva-portal.org/smash/get/diva2:1611997/FULLTEXT01.pdf

Bjørn, A., & Hauschild, M. Z. (2015). Introducing carrying capacity-based normalisation in LCA: framework and development of references at midpoint level. The International Journal of Life Cycle Assessment. https://link.springer.com/article/10.1007/s11367-015-0899-2

Bjørn, A., Chandrakumar, C., Boulay, A.-M., Doka, G., Fang, K., Gondran, N., Hauschild, M.Z., Kerkhof, A., King, H., Margni, M., McLaren, S., Mueller, C., Owsianiak, M., Peters, G., Roos, S., Sala, S., Sandin, G., Sim, S., Vargas-Gonzalez, M. & Ryberg, M. (2020). Review of life-cycle based methods for absolute environmental sustainability assessment and their applications. Environmental Research Letters 15(8): 083001. DOI 10.1088/1748-9326/ab89d7

Bolig- og Planstyrelsen. (2022). Klimakrav (LCA) i Bygningsreglementet. Bolig- og Planstyrelsen. https://bpst.dk/da/Byggeri/Baeredygtigt-byggeri/NY-Klimakrav-i-bygningsreglementet#introduktion

Breyer, C., Fasihi, M., Bajamundi, C., & Creutzig, F. (2019). Direct Air Capture of CO2 : A Key Technology for Ambitious Climate Change Mitigation. https://doi.org/10.1016/j.joule.2019.08.010

Broekhoff, D., Gillenwater, M., Colbert-Sangree, T., & Cage, P. (2019). Securing Climate Benefit: A Guide to Using Carbon Offsets. https://www.offsetguide.org/

Buis, A. (2019). The atmosphere: Getting a handle on carbon dioxide – climate change: Vital signs of the planet. NASA. https://climate.nasa.gov/news/2915/the-atmosphere-getting-a-handle-on-carbon-dioxide/

Chouinard, Y. (2022). Earth is now our only shareholder. Patagonia. https://www.patagonia.com/ownership/

Common Objective. (2021). WFTO inside view: Manos del uruguay. Common Objective. https://www.commonobjective.co/article/wfto-inside-view-manos-del-uruguay

Crawford, R. H., & Pullen, S. (2011). Life cycle water analysis of a residential building and its occupants. ResearchGate. https://www.researchgate.net/publication/233239036_Life_cycle_water_analysis_of_a_residential_building_and_its_occupants

Danmarks Statistik, 2030-Panelet. (2020). Gør Verdensmål til Vores Mål: 197 danske målepunkter for en mere bæredygtig verden. https://realdania.dk/publikationer/faglige-publikationer/indoor-climate-and-healt-in-homes

Dansgaard, W., Johnsen, S. J., Clausen, H. B., Dahl-Jensen, D., Gundestrup, N. S., Hammer, C. U., Hvidberg, C. S., Steffensen, J. P., Sveinbjörnsdottir, A. E., Jouzel, J., & Bond, G. (1993). Evidence for general instability of past climate from a 250-kyr ice-core record. Nature News. https://www.nature.com/articles/364218a0

DEAL. (2022). Doughnut Design for Business - Core Tool. Doughnut Economics Action Lab. https://doughnuteconomics.org/tools/191

DEAL. (2022). Doughnut Unrolled: Introducing the four lenses. Doughnut Economics Action Lab. https://doughnuteconomics.org/tools/142

Denchak, M. (2018). Building a Healthy Home. NRDC.

https://www.nrdc.org/stories/building-healthy-home

Ducros, A., & Steele, P. (2022). Biocredits to finance nature and people - Emerging lessons. www.iied.org

Energistyrelsen (2022). Global Arapportering 2022. Energistyrelsen. https://ens.dk/sites/ens.dk/files/Basisfremskrivning/ga22_-_hovedrapport.pdf
European Union. (2006). Regulation (EC) No 166/2006 of the European Parliament and of the Council of 18 January 2006 concerning the establishment of a European Pollutant Release and Transfer Register and amending Council Directives 91/689/EEC and 96/61/EC (Text with EEA relevance). https://eur-lex.europa.eu/EN/legal-content/summary/european-pollutant-release-and-transfer-register-e-prtr.html

Faith In Nature. (2022). A vote for nature. Faith In Nature. https://www.faithinnature.co.uk/pages/avotefornature

Fajardy, M., & Dowell, N. M. (2017). Can BECCS deliver sustainable and resource efficient negative emissions? Energy and Environmental Science, 10(6), 1389–1426. https://doi.org/10.1039/c7ee00465f

Fanning, A.L. and Hickel, J. (2023). Compensation for atmospheric appropriation, Nature Sustainability, in press. https://doi.org/10.1038/s41893-023-01130-8

Fasihi, M., Efimova, O., & Breyer, C. (2019). Techno-economic assessment of CO2 direct air capture plants. Journal of Cleaner Production, 224, 957–980. https://doi.org/10.1016/j.jclepro.2019.03.086

Fawzy, S., Osman, A. I., Yang, H., Doran, J., & Rooney, D. W. (2021). Industrial biochar systems for atmospheric carbon removal: a review. In Environmental Chemistry Letters (Vol. 19, Issue 4, pp. 3023–3055). Springer Science and Business Media Deutschland GmbH. https://doi.org/10.1007/s10311-021-01210-1

Haberl, H., K. Heinz Erb, Krausmann, F, Gaube, V., Bondeau, A., Plutzar, C., Gingrich, S., Lucht, W., and Fischer-Kowalsk, M. (2007). Quantifying and mapping the human appropriation of net primary production in earth'sterrestrial ecosystems. PNAS vol. 104, no. 31, pp. 12942-12947. https://www.pnas.org/doi/epdf/10.1073/pnas.0704243104

Hahn, T., Koh, N. S., & Elmqvist, T. (2022). No net loss of biodiversity, green growth, and the need to address drivers. In One Earth (Vol. 5, Issue 6, pp. 612–614). Cell Press. https://doi.org/10.1016/j.oneear.2022.05.022

Hartmann, J., West, A. J., Renforth, P., Köhler, P., de La Rocha, C. L., Wolf-Gladrow, D. A., Dürr, H. H., & Scheffran, J. (2013). Enhanced chemical weathering as a geoengineering strategy to reduce atmospheric carbon dioxide, supply nutrients, and mitigate ocean acidification. Reviews of Geophysics, 51(2), 113–149. https://doi.org/10.1002/rog.20004

Häyhä, T., Lucas, P.L., van Vuuren, D.P., Cornell, S.E. & Hoff, H. (2016). From Planetary Boundaries to national fair shares of the global safe operating space — How can the scales be bridged? Global Environmental Change 40: 60–72. https://doi.org/10.1016/j.gloenvcha.2016.06.008

Huijbregts, M. A. J., Steinmann, Z. J. N., Elshout, P. M. F., Stam, G., Verones, F., Vieira, M., Zijp, M., Hollander, A., & van Zelm, R. (2017). ReCiPe2016: a harmonised life cycle impact assessment method at midpoint and endpoint level. International Journal of Life Cycle Assessment, 22(2), 138–147. https://doi.org/10.1007/s11367-016-1246-y

Krausmann, F., Erb, K.-H., Gingrich, S., Haberl, H., Bondeau, A., Gaube, V., Lauk, C., Plutzar, C., & Searchinger, T. D. (2013). Global human appropriation of net primary production doubled in the 20th century. https://www.pnas.org/doi/10.1073/pnas.121134911

IPCC. (2022). Climate Change 2022: Mitigation of Climate Change. Intergovernmental Panel on Climate Change. https://www.ipcc.ch/report/ar6/wg3/downloads/report/IPCC_AR6_WGIII_FullReport.pdf

Jensen, K. G., Birgisdottir, H., Poulsgaard, K. S., Lind, L., Christensen, C. Ø., Skjelmose, O., Carruth, S. J., Jensen, K. K., Canera, I. O., Manbodh, J., & Zimmermann, R. K. (2018). Guide to Sustainable Building Certifications. Aalborg University's Research Portal. https://vbn.aau.dk/en/publications/guide-to-sustainable-building-certifications

Lucas, P.L., Wilting, H.C., Hof, A.F. & van Vuuren, D.P. (2020). Allocating planetary boundaries to large economies: Distributional consequences of alternative perspectives on distributive fairness. Global Environmental Change 60: 102017. https://doi.org/10.1016/j.gloenvcha.2019.102017

Millward-Hopkins, J., Steinberger, J. K., Rao, N. D., & Oswald, Y. (2020). Providing decent living with minimum energy: A global scenario. Global Environmental Change, 65. https://doi.org/10.1016/j.gloenvcha.2020.102168

Mora, C., Tittensor, D. P., Adl, S., Simpson, A. G. B., & Worm, B. (2011). How Man Species Are There on Earth and in the Ocean. https://journals.plos.org/plosbiology/article/file?type=printable&id=10.1371/journal.pbio.1001127

Panks, S. A., White, N. A., Newsome, A. A., Nash, M. A., Potter, J. A., Heydon, M. A., Mayhew, E. A., Alvarez, M. A., Russell, T. A., Cashon, C. A., Goddard, F. A., Scott B, S. J., Heaver, M. C., Scott C, S. H., Treweek, J. D., Butcher, B. E., & Stone, D. A. (2022). Biodiversity metric 3.1: Auditing and accounting for biodiversity - User Guide. https://publications.naturalengland.org.uk/publication/6049804846366720

Persson, L., Almroth, B. M. C., Collins, C. D., Cornell, S., Wit, C. A. d., Diamond, M. L., Fantke, P., Hassellöv, M., MacLeod, M., Ryberg, M. W., Jørgensen, P. S., Villarrubia-Gómez, P., Wang, Z., & Hauschild, M. Z. (2022). Outside the Safe Operating Space of the Planetary Boundary for Novel Entities. Environmental Science & Technology 2022 56 (3), 1510-1521. http://doi.org/10.1021/acs.est.1c04158

Petersen, S., Ryberg, M. W., & Birkved, M. (2022). The safe operating space for greenhouse gas emissions. https://doi.org/10.48550/arXiv.2209.00118

Petit, J. R., Jouzel, J., Raynaud, D., Barkov, N. I., Barnola, J.-M., Basile, I., Bender, M., Chappellaz, J., Davis, M., Delaygue, G., Delmotte, M., Kotlyakov, V. M., Legrand, M., Lipenkov, V. Y., Lorius, C., PÉpin, L., Ritz, C., Saltzman, E., & Stievenard, M. (1999). Climate and atmospheric history of the past 420,000 years from the Vostok Ice Core, Antarctica. Nature News. https://www.nature.com/articles/20859

Raworth, K. (2012). A safe and just space for humanity: Can we live within the doughnut? Oxfam. https://oi-files-d8-prod.s3.eu-west-2.amazonaws.com/s3fs-public/file_attachments/dp-a-safe-and-just-space-for-humanity-130212-en_5.pdf

Raworth, K. (2017). Doughnut Economics: Seven Ways to Think Like a 21st-Century Economist.

Raworth, K., Krestyaninova, O., Eriksson, F., Feibusch, L., Sanz, C., Benyus, J., Dwyer, J., Miller, N. H., Douma, A., Laak, I. t., Raspail, N., Ehlers, L., & Lipton, J. (2020). The Amsterdam City Doughnut. Doughnut Economics Action Lab, Biomimicry 3.8, Circle Economy & C40 Cities. https://www.kateraworth.com/wp/wp-content/uploads/2020/04/20200416-AMS-portrait-EN-

Spread-web-420x210mm.pdf

Realdania. (2019). Indoor Climate and Health in Homes. Realdania. https://realdania.dk/publikationer/faglige-publikationer/indoor-climate-and-healt-in-homes

Reduction Roadmap (2022) Reduction Roadmap: Preconditions and Methodologies. Version 2 - 7 September, 2022. www.reductionroadmap.dk.

Rockström, J., Steffen, W., Noone, K., Persson, Å., Chapin, F. S. I., Lambin, E., Lenton, T., Scheffer, M., Folke, C., Schellnhuber, H. J., Nykvist, B., de Wit, C., Hughes, T., van der Leeuw, S., Rodhe, H., Sörlin, S., Snyder, P., Costanza, R., Svedin, U., … Foley, J. (2009). Planetary boundaries: Exploring the safe operating space for humanity. Ecology and Society. https://www.ecologyandsociety.org/vol14/iss2/art32/

Ryberg, M.W., Andersen, M.M., Owsianiak, M. & M.Z. Hauschild. (2020). Downscaling the planetary boundaries in absolute environmental sustainability assessments – A review. Journal of Cleaner Production 276: 123287. https://doi.org/10.1016/j.jclepro.2020.123287

Ryberg, M. W., Owsianiak, M., Richardson, K., & Hauschild, M. Z. (2018). Development of a life-cycle impact assessment methodology linked to the Planetary Boundaries framework. Ecological Indicators, 88, 250–262. https://doi.org/10.1016/j.ecolind.2017.12.065

Scholes, R., Biggs, R. (2005). A biodiversity intactness index. Nature 434, 45–49. https://doi.org/10.1038/nature03289

Sizirici, B., Fseha, Y., Cho, C.-S., Yildiz, I., & Byon, Y.-J. (2021). A review of carbon footprint reduction in construction industry, from design to operation. https://www.ncbi.nlm.nih.gov/pmc/articles/PMC8540435/

Steffen, W., Richardson, K., Rockström, J., Cornell, S. E., Fetzer, I., Bennett, E. M., Biggs, R., Carpenter, S. R., de Vries, W., de Wit, C. A., Folke, C., Gerten, D., Heinke, J., Mace, G. M., Persson, L. M., Ramanathan, V., Reyers, B., & Sörlin, S. (2015). Planetary boundaries: Guiding human development on a changing planet. Science, 347(6223). https://doi.org/10.1126/science.1259855

Stocker, T.F., Qin, D., Plattner, G.-K., Tignor, M., Allen, S.K., Boschung, J., Nauels, A., Xia, Y., Bex, V. & Midgley, P.M. (2013). Climate Change 2013: The Physical Science Basis. Contribution of Working Group I to the Fifth Assessment Report of the Intergovernmental Panel on Climate Change. Cambridge University Press. https://www.ipcc.ch/report/ar5/wg1/

Stoknes, P.E. & Rockström, J. (2018). Redefining green growth within planetary boundaries. https://doi.org/10.1016/j.erss.2018.04.030

UK government. (2023). Guidance: Biodiversity metric: calculate the biodiversity net gain of a project or development. Department for Environment, Food & Rural Affairs. https://www.gov.uk/guidance/biodiversity-metric-calculate-the-biodiversity-net-gain-of-a-project-or-development

UN-Habitat. (2022). Envisaging the Future of Cities. World Cities Report 2022. https://unhabitat.org/sites/default/files/2022/06/wcr_2022.pdf

United Nations. (1987). Multilateral - Montreal Protocol on Substances that Deplete the Ozone Layer. https://treaties.un.org/doc/Publication/UNTS/Volume%201522/volume-1522-I-26369-English.pdf

van den Berg, N. J., van Soest, H. L., Hof, A. F., den Elzen, M. G. J., van Vuuren, D. P., Chen, W., Drouet, L., Emmerling, J., Fujimori, S., Höhne, N., Kõberle, A. C., McCollum, D., Schaeffer, R., Shekhar, S., Vishwanathan,

S. S., Vrontisi, Z., & Blok, K. (2020). Implications of various effort-sharing approaches for national carbon budgets and emission pathways. Climatic Change, 162(4), 1805–1822. https://doi.org/10.1007/s10584-019-02368-y

Velux. (2022). Healthy Homex Barometer 2022: Sustainable building for a resilient society. Velux Group. https://velcdn.azureedge.net/-/media/com/healthy-homes-barometer/hhb-2022/velux-hhb-report-2022.pdf

Villarrubia-Gómez, P., Cornell, S. E., & Fabres, J. (2018). Marine plastic pollution as a planetary boundary threat – the drifting piece in the Sustainability Puzzle. ScienceDirect. https://www.sciencedirect.com/science/article/pii/S0308597X17305456

Wang-Erlandsson, L., Tobian, A., van der Ent, R. J., Fetzer, I., te Wierik, S., Porkka, M., Staal, A., Jaramillo, F., Dahlmann, H., Singh, C., Greve, P., Gerten, D., Keys, P. W., Gleeson, T., Cornell, S. E., Steffen, W., Bai, X., & Rockström, J. (2022). A planetary boundary for Green Water. Nature News. https://www.nature.com/articles/s43017-022-00287-8

Willicroft. (2022). Our Impact: Mother Nature CEO. Willicroft. https://willicroft.com/our-impact

Wilson, A. (2011). Greensulate – A fungus-based insultation material that's grown rather than manufactured. Building Green. https://www.buildinggreen.com/blog/greensulate---fungus-based-insulation-material-thats-grown-rather-manufactured

World Health Organization. (2022). Household air pollution. World Health Organization. https://www.who.int/news-room/fact-sheets/detail/household-air-pollution-and-health

Zimmermann, R. K., Andersen, C. M. E., Kanafani, K., Birgisdottir, H. (2021). Whole Life Carbon Assessment of 60 buildings: Possibilities to develop benchmark values for LCA of buildings. Aalborg Universitet. https://sbi.dk/Pages/Whole-Life-Carbon-Assessment-of-60-buildings.aspx

Organisations, certifications, standards, frameworks and tools

4 til 1 planet. (2022). Byggeriets CO2-aftryk skal meget længere ned, hvis klimaforandringerne skal bremses. Retrieved 2023, from https://www.4til1planet.dk/nyheder/byggeriets-co2-aftrykhttps://amul.com/m/a-note-on-the-achievements-of-the-dairy-cooperatives

Amul.com. (n.d.). A note on the achievements of the Dairy Cooperatives. Amul. Retrieved 2023, from https://amul.com/m/a-note-on-the-achievements-of-the-dairy-cooperatives

B Lab. (n.d.). B Impact Assessment. Retrieved 2023, from https://www.bcorporation.net/en-us/programs-and-tools/b-impact-assessment/

BRE Group. (n.d.). BREEAM is the world's leading science-based suite of validation and certification systems for sustainable built environment. Retrieved 2023, from https://bregroup.com/products/breeam/

Dansk Standard (2019). DS/EN 15804:2012+A2:2019: Sustainability of construction works – Environmental product declarations – Core rules for the product category of construction products.

European Commission. (2023). Corporate sustainability reporting. Retrieved 2023, from https://finance.ec.europa.eu/capital-markets-union-and-financial-markets/company-reporting-and-auditing/company-reporting/corporate-sustainability-reporting_en

European Commission. (2020). EU Taxonomy.

Retrieved 2023, from https://ec.europa.eu/sustainable-finance-taxonomy/home

European Commission. (2019). Sustainability-related disclosure in the financial services sector. Retrieved 2023, from https://finance.ec.europa.eu/sustainable-finance/disclosures/sustainability-related-disclosure-financial-services-sector_en

German Sustainable Building Council. (n.d.). The DGNB System. Retrieved 2023, from https://www.dgnb-system.de/en/system/index.php

Global Impact Investing Network (n.d.). IRIS+ is the generally accepted system for measuring, managing, and optimizing impact. Retrieved 2023, from https://iris.thegiin.org/

Global Reporting Initiative. (n.d.). The global leader for impact reporting. Retrieved 2023, from https://www.globalreporting.org/

Gold Standard (n.d.). We manage best practice standards for climate and sustainable development interventions to maximise impact, creating value for people around the world and the planet we share. Retrieved 2023, from https://www.goldstandard.org/about-us/vision-and-mission

GRESB. (n.d.). About us: GRESB, the global ESG benchmark. Retrieved 2023, from https://www.gresb.com/nl-en/

International WELL Being Institute. (n.d.). About IWBI – People-First Places. Retrieved 2023, from https://www.wellcertified.com/about-iwbi/

Klimate.co (n.d.). Carbon removal. Retrieved 2023, from https://klimate.co/carbon-removal/

LCA for Experts (GaBi) (n.d.). LCA for Experts Software built on the world's most robust LCA databases. Retrieved 2023, from https://sphera.com/life-cycle-assessment-lca-software

LCAbyg (n.d.). About LCAbyg: LCAbyg is a tool that calculates life cycle assessments for buildings. Retrieved 2023, from https://www.lcabyg.dk/en/

One Click LCA (n.d.). World's fastest building life cycle assessment software. Retrieved 2023, from https://www.oneclicklca.com/

OpenLCA (n.d.). The world's leading, high performance, open source Life Cycle Assessment software. Retrieved 2023, from https://www.openlca.org/

Opwall (n.d.). The Wallacea Trust: Business solutions for environmental challenges. Retrieved 2023, from https://www.opwall.com/the-wallacea-trust/

ÖKOBAUDAT (n.d.). Sustainable Construction Information Portal. German Federal Ministry for Housing, Urban Development and Building (BMWSB). Retrieved 2023, from https://www.oekobaudat.de/no_cache/en/database/search/daten/db2.html#bereich2

Plan Vivo Foundation (n.d.). What we do. Retrieved 2023, from https://www.planvivo.org/what-we-do

Reduction Roadmap (2022). Reduction Roadmap: Preconditions and Methodologies. Retrieved 2023, from https://www.reductionroadmap.dk

REScoop. (n.d.). The RESCOOP model. ReScoop. Retrieved 2023, from https://www.rescoop.eu/the-rescoop-model

Rådet for Bæredygtigt Byggeri (2023). DGNB Udmærkelse: DGNB Planet. Retrieved 2023, from

https://rfbb.dk/dgnb-udmaerkelse/167161412883
5x720381061232328700

SimaPro (n.d.). LCA software for informed change-makers. Retrieved 2023, from https://simapro.com/

Terrasos (n.d.). About Terrasos. Retrieved 2023, from

https://en.terrasos.co/sobre-terrasos

UN Global Compact. (n.d.). SDG Action Manager. United Nations Global Compact. Retrieved 2023, from https://unglobalcompact.org/take-action/sdg-action-manager

United Nations. (2015). The 17 goals. United Nations. Retrieved 2023, from https://sdgs.un.org/goals

USGBC. (n.d.). LEED rating system: The most widely used green building rating system. Retrieved 2023, from https://www.usgbc.org/leed

ValueNature. (n.d.). Developing blockchain underpinned biodiversity credits for the voluntary market. Retrieved 2023, from https://valuenature.earth/

VERRA (n.d.). Verra sets the world's leading standards for climate action and sustainable development. Retrieved 2023, from https://verra.org/about/overview/

Building cases:

Hammarby Sjöstad
https://vaxer.stockholm/omraden/stadsutvecklingsomrade-hammarby-sjostad/
Photo credit: Tina Li's mom <3

Tingbjerhuse
https://vandkunsten.com/projects/fortolker-og-fortaetter-arkitekturarv
Photo credit: Vandkunsten

Veligbolig Plus
https://onv.dk/projekt/venligbolig-plus/
Photo credit: ONV

The Circl ABN AMBRO Pavilion
https://circl.nl/themakingof/en/
Photo credit: Architekten Cie

The Swan
https://lendager.com/project/the-swan/
Photo credit: Architekten Cie

Velux Living Places
https://buildforlife.velux.com/en/livingplaces
Photo credit: EFFEKT

CPH Village Jenbanebyen
https://arcgency.com/cph-village-vesterbro
Photo credit: Architekten Cie

Kajstaden Tall Timber Building
https://www.cfmoller.com/p/Kajstaden-Tall-Timber-Building-i3592.html
Photo credit: C.F. Møller

Photo credit:

Publication Images, Rasmus Hjortshøj
Portrait of Kate Raworth, RomanKrznaric
Portrait of Kasper Guldager Jensen, Tom Jersø

Contributing experts: Anjila Hjalsted, Christina Wikberger, Christine Collin, Christoffer Søholm Kristensen, Erik Andersson, Feodora Frisesdal, Frederik Brauer, Jasper Strømgren, Klara Faldborg, Klara Lauridsen, Lau Raffnsøe, Liv Stranddorf, Niak Sian Koh, Rasmus Søgaard, Rasmus Juul-Nyholm, Simon Kofod-Svendsen, Søren Nielsen, Tiina Häyhä, Trine Bentzen and Tue Foged.

Contributing organisations: Aalborg University - BUILD, Danish Technical University, Doughnut Economic Action Lab (DEAL), Green Building Council - Denmark, EFFEKT, Home.Earth, SLA, Sweco, Stockholm Resilience Centre and Vandkunsten

Co-creators

Anders Bjørn
Allocation Principles

Andrew Fanning
Doughnut Economics

Artur Branny
Planetary Boundaries

Caroline Clausen
Allocation Principles

Dan Pham
Impact Design

Emil Engelbrecht
Graphic Design

Emil Bender Lassen
Impact Design

Enrich Sahan
Doughnut Economics

Frederik Moberg
Planetary Boundaries

Harpa Birgisdóttir
Life Cycle Assessment

Ingo Fetzer
Planetary Boundaries

Jonathan Leonardsen
Social Impact

Kate Raworth
Doughnut Economics

Kristine K. Rasmussen
Biodiversity

Leonora Grcheva
Doughnut Economics

Mie Heide
Social Impact

Morten Ryberg
Allocation Principles

Nicolas Francart
Life Cycle Assessment

Rasmus Nørgaard
Business Design

Tina Li
Illustration

Doughnut for Urban Development / Manual

The Doughnut for Urban Development Manual is available for free, by digital download in both Danish and English. Please share it with relevant stakeholders in your professional network.

Doughnut for Urban Development / Appendix

The Doughnut for Urban Development Appendix is available for free, by digital download in both Danish and English. The Appendix includes deep dives into the content described throughout this book. This is where you can find the 'Off-Site Biodiversity Tool.'

Doughnut for Urban Development / Database

Doughnut for Urban Development Database is the detailed frameworks and references behind the impact areas described in the social foundation and ecological ceiling. You can download for free and adjust as you build your own library of impact indicators.

Doughnut for Urban Development / Toolkit

Doughnut for Urban Development Toolkit follows the 'Doughnut Unrolled' methodology and can be used to facilitate workshops with relevant stakeholders in your next urban development project.